teen's
guides

LIVING
with
SPORTS
INJURIES

Also in the
Teen's Guides series

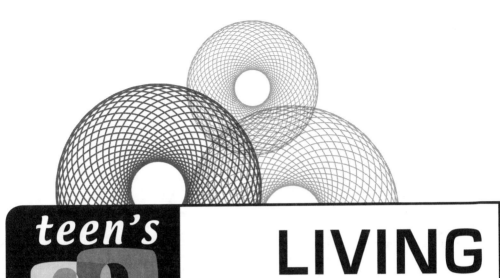

LIVING
with
SPORTS
INJURIES

Clifford D. Stark, D.O.
with Elizabeth Shimer Bowers

Checkmark Books®
An imprint of Infobase Publishing

Living with Sports Injuries

Copyright © 2010 by Clifford D. Stark, D.O.

Checkmark Books
An imprint of Infobase Publishing, Inc.
132 West 31st Street
New York NY 10001

Library of Congress Cataloging-in-Publication Data

Stark, Clifford D.
  Living with sports injuries / by Clifford D. Stark ; with Elizabeth Shimer Bowers.
      p. cm. — (Teen's guides)
  Includes bibliographical references and index.
    ISBN-13: 978-0-8160-7848-6 (hardcover : alk. paper)
    ISBN-10: 0-8160-7848-3 (hardcover : alk. paper)
    ISBN-13: 978-0-8160-7849-3 (pbk. : alk. paper)
    ISBN-10: 0-8160-7849-1 (pbk. : alk. paper) 1. Sports injuries—Popular works.
I. Bowers, Elizabeth Shimer. II. Title.
  RD97.S825 2010
  617.1'027—dc22   2009026712

Checkmark Books are available at special discounts when purchased in bulk quantities for businesses, associations, institutions or sales promotions. Please call our Special Sales Department in New York at (212) 967-8800 or (800) 322-8755.

You can find Facts On File on the World Wide Web at http://www.factsonfile.com

Excerpts included herewith have been reprinted by permission of the copyright holders; the author has made every effort to contact copyright holders. The publishers will be glad to rectify, in future editions, any errors or omissions brought to their notice.

Text design by Annie O'Donnell
Composition by Hermitage Publishing Services
Cover printed by Art Print, Taylor, Pa.
Book printed and bound by Maple-Vail Book Manufacturing Group, York, Pa.
Date printed: April 2010
Printed in the United States of America

10 9 8 7 6 5 4 3 2 1

This book is printed on acid-free paper.

CONTENTS

A Crash Course in Sports Injuries

Aaron, age 16, is the second-best runner on his high school cross-country team. But during the last few practices, Aaron slowed slightly, due to a nagging pain in his leg. After a trip to his family doctor, he learned that the pain is not due to shin splints, as he had thought; instead, he has a *stress fracture*. Aaron's doctor has advised him to refrain from running for the next six weeks, but Aaron's coach is urging him to run in the upcoming meet—against their rival team—and then start his rest period. Aaron is upset for a number of reasons: He is disappointed about his injury, restless because he knows he will have to take a break from running during the peak of his competitive season, nervous about letting down both his team and his coach, and afraid to go against his coach's request that he still compete despite his doctor's orders.

Unfortunately, Aaron's situation is all too common. Injuries are quite prevalent among high school athletes; each year, approximately 30 million students participate in organized sports in the United States, and an estimated 20 percent experience sports-related musculoskeletal injuries. And by virtue of being a teen, Aaron is more at-risk for sports injuries than an adult athlete: Teens grow rapidly during puberty, which puts them at an increased risk for several exercise-related injuries.

Although most coaches are supportive of necessary rest periods, a select few—such as Aaron's—are not. Knowing how best to deal with this type of coach will help speed healing and prevent future injury. This book can help.

AN INTRODUCTION TO SPORTS INJURIES

As a teenager, participation in sports and physical activity is a wonderful way to spend your time. Not only will you get your body in shape, improve your coordination, and engage you in healthy competition, you will form enriching relationships with your teammates and coaches. However, by virtue of participating in a sport, you also put yourself at risk for injury.

This chapter will provide an overview of sports injuries in teens—why they happen, where on the body they can occur, and what teen athletes can do to prevent and treat them. It will also discuss how injuries make teenage athletes prone to reinjury due to weakness of the muscles and ligaments in the area that was hurt.

In addition, this chapter will offer tips on how teen athletes like Aaron can talk to their coaches about their injuries and handle the "middleman" role between their physicians and coaches when it comes to the decision of whether or not they should play.

Sports injuries come in many forms, but they fall into two general categories—*overuse injuries* and *acute injuries.*

Overuse injuries occur when muscles, tendons, growth plates, or bones cannot keep up with the stress put on them, so they break down and cause pain. These types of injuries tend to occur in sports with repetitive motions, such as gymnastics, running, tennis, soccer, dance, and baseball. If you practice your sport all year round, or you play multiple sports in the same season, you are at an increased risk for overuse injuries. Specifically, teen athletes who train more than 10 to 12 hours per week, play in games more than three times a week, or have had a recent increase in exercise intensity, duration, or frequency are at an elevated risk for these types of injuries.

At first, pain with an overuse injury typically occurs only during the activity that caused it; later, it also starts to hurt when you're not practicing your sport, during your normal daily activities, or even at rest.

Acute sports injuries, on the other hand, usually occur after a sudden trauma. For instance, they may occur as a result of a twisted ankle on the soccer field, a fall during a football game, or a collision with another player on the basketball court. Acute sports injuries in teens commonly include *bruises* (also called contusions), *sprains* (also called partial or complete ligament tears), *strains* (also called partial or complete tears of muscles or tendons), and *fractures.*

PREVENTING SPORTS INJURIES

Most teens have probably heard the expression, "Don't merely play a sport to get in shape; get in shape to play a sport." Sure, sports like football, basketball, and cross-country are great forms of exercise, but it is also important for young athletes to stay in shape and participate in the right kind of training to do well in their sports and prevent injuries at the same time.

One of the best ways to deal with sports injuries is to prevent them in the first place, and an effective way to prevent injuries is to stay in shape. That's right—even if you play a low-impact sport such as golf, good overall general conditioning will help you avoid injury.

Specifically, effective conditioning will help strengthen your heart, lungs, and musculoskeletal system, and it will help reduce body fat, improve balance and coordination, and make you more flexible. Proper conditioning includes stretching, endurance training, and strength training.

In general, physical activity falls into one of two categories: *aerobic activity* and *anaerobic activity*.

AEROBIC ACTIVITY

The word *aerobic* means "with oxygen." Aerobic conditioning involves activities that increase your heart rate, and therefore, strengthen your cardiovascular system. Because your cells need oxygen to burn fat, aerobic activities such as swimming, cycling, and jogging help your muscles burn fat for energy. By strengthening your cardiovascular system, aerobic exercise helps your heart to pump blood with fewer beats and your lungs to process air more easily, both of which give more blood to your muscles and organs and make injuries less likely. In addition, aerobic activity boosts your energy level, allows you to play your sport longer without getting tired, improves your muscle tone, helps control your weight, reduces stress, and helps you sleep better—all of which help protect you against injuries.

For maximum benefits, some experts recommend you do some sort of aerobic activity, be it jogging, swimming, biking, or brisk walking for 30 to 60 minutes most days of the week at 70 to 85 percent of your *maximum heart rate*, although some studies show that you get the same benefits from exercising less often than this. The most important thing is that you get regular aerobic exercise at least a few times a week for a minimum of 20 minutes at a time. In terms of heart rate, exercising below your *target heart rate* will not yield significant benefits, and exercising above your target heart rate may put you at risk for strain or injury.

To calculate your maximum heart rate, take 220 minus your age. For example, if you are 17 years old, your maximum heart rate is 203 beats per minute (BPM). Then, to calculate your target heart rate, take 70 to 85 percent of your maximum; if your maximum heart rate is 203 BPM, your target heart rate will be between 142 and 172 BPM.

To monitor your heart rate, you can buy a heart rate monitor (they cost between $150 and $350), or you can simply take your own pulse (which is free).

To take your pulse, place your index and middle fingers on the underside of your wrist (on your radial artery) or the side of your neck on either side of your windpipe (on your carotid artery). Count your pulse for 15 seconds and multiply it by four to get your heart rate per minute. If you are within your target heart rate range, you should continue to exercise at your current pace. If you are below it, you should increase the intensity. If you are above it, you should pull back. Also keep in mind that your target heart rate will give you only an idea of how hard your body is working—if you feel dizzy or faint, or if something starts to hurt, you should decrease your intensity.

ANAEROBIC ACTIVITY

Anaerobic exercises, such as weight lifting and sprinting, are done without the use of oxygen. Instead of fat, anaerobic activities burn carbohydrates for fuel. You will get some indirect fat-burning benefits from anaerobic activities, however; because they increase your overall metabolism, anaerobic exercises do contribute to fat burning in the long run.

In addition to sufficient physical conditioning, here are some ways you can help prevent sports injuries.

Warm up before practices and competitions. Warm your muscles by jogging in place, riding a stationary bike, or jumping rope for about three to five minutes. When you warm up by doing light activities before your main exercise routine, it raises your body temperature slightly, which helps warm your muscle fibers. Warm muscles are softer, stronger, and less likely to pull or tear. Warming up also lubricates your joints, which helps them move more freely with less energy expenditure and protects them from excessive wear. You will know you have warmed up sufficiently when you break a sweat; when your body starts sweating, it means you have raised your temperature about two degrees.

Cool down after you have finished exercising. Once you have completed your workout or training routine, you should continue to move for five to 10 minutes at a slower pace with slow jogging or walking. Cooling down helps transport oxygen-rich blood to your brain and other organs, and it prevents the muscle cramps, nausea, and dizziness that can sometimes set in after exercise. It also enhances the removal of lactic acid from your muscles, helping to prevent soreness.

Stretch, and then stretch again. Whether you are a runner, swimmer, dancer, or tennis player, stretching is important. For best results, you should stretch often, always after you warm up, and then again at the end of your practice or competition, after you cool down. Stretching at the proper times—when your body is warm, and before and after your main exercise—is very important. A cross-country runner who rolls out of bed in the morning and immediately starts stretching risks tearing her muscles. If she stretches after she has warmed up for a few minutes, however, she will help lengthen her muscles and improve the range of motion of her muscles and joints. To stretch properly, stretch gradually and gently; perform a static stretch, holding each muscle still for 10 to 20 seconds. As you stretch, imagine your muscles becoming softer and more flexible. Avoid bouncing stretches, which can actually shorten the muscle fibers and do more harm than not stretching at all. Aim for a total of 10 to 20 minutes of stretching time after both your warm-up and cooldown. Although it may be tempting to skip your stretches when you are in a hurry, keep in mind that your stretching time may be the most important part of your workout—stretching is a powerful tool against injuries, soreness, and stiffness.

Strength train. If you are a runner or a swimmer, you might think, "Why do *I* need to lift weights?" But the truth is that strength training is an important part of overall good athletic conditioning, and it can benefit any athlete, from a defensive back on a football team to a cheerleader on the sidelines. To be most effective, weight training should be adjusted to meet the requirements of your sport. For example, if you are a linebacker on the football team, you will need to improve both upper and lower body strength to make your tackles. If you are a running back, you should concentrate on lower body strength training to develop your legs. Strength training is equally as important for female athletes as it is for males, particularly when it comes to strengthening the upper body. Talk to your coach or the physical trainer at your school about developing a strength training program that matches your individual sport, and if applicable, your specific position on the team.

Stay hydrated by drinking sufficient water or sports drinks. If you are dehydrated, you will feel tired and be less coordinated, both of which will make you more likely to get injured. Warning signs of dehydration include thirstiness (once you feel thirsty, it indicates that you already have a water deficit), headache, dark-colored urine, and weakness. If you experience any of these signs during exercise, stop activity immediately, drink fluids, and eat a light snack. To prevent dehydration in the first place, you should drink at least eight to 10 glasses of water or sports drinks per day, and more on days that you train or compete. If you are sweating a lot, make sure you drink one to 1.5 liters of fluid per hour of intense activity. To avoid the stomach cramps that can result from drinking too much at once, pace yourself with a cup of water or sports drink every 15 to 20 minutes. You should also drink fluids before and after periods of exercise. Drinking adequate fluids is even more important if you are going to compete or train in hot weather, when your body loses more water and thus is more at-risk for dehydration. You should avoid drinking liquids that contain alcohol or caffeine, as they can increase fluid loss and put you at greater risk of dehydration.

Cross train. Cross-training—or participating in aerobic activities other than your sport—is a great way to tone different muscle groups and take some of the strain off the muscles you use during your chosen sport. Cross-training is particularly helpful in reducing the risk of injury that comes with repetitive motions in sports such as running and gymnastics. Effective, joint-friendly cross-training activities include low-impact forms of aerobic exercise such as biking and swimming, weight training, and flexibility exercises like yoga and Pilates. These activities can be done in place of your sport in the seasons you take off, and they can be performed in addition to your sport in the season(s) when you are competing.

Diversify. If you play the same sport all year round, you will put yourself at risk for an overuse injury. To develop different muscles and different skills, play different sports in different seasons. Not only will this help you become a more well-rounded person overall, it will make you a more effective athlete. For example: Play soccer in the fall; run winter track in the winter; play baseball in the spring. Also, if possible, avoid playing more than one sport per season—participating in multiple sports at the same time will also put you at risk for injury.

Use appropriate protective devices for your sport. Safety gear is sport-specific and includes goggles, mouth guards, elbow, knee, and shin pads, and helmets. For instance, if you play football, use pads and helmets that fit you well. If you play baseball, wear helmets and gloves as needed. If you play field hockey, wear shin and mouth guards. If you run, make sure you wear running shoes that offer sufficient support and padding. No matter what type of protective gear you use, make sure it fits you properly.

If you suspect you may have an injury, see a doctor right away.

TREATING SPORTS INJURIES

No matter how a sports injury occurred or where on your body it took place, it's important that you start to take care of it as soon as possible. Depending on the severity of the injury, with proper rest and treatment, you may be able to continue participating in your sport through the season. If you ignore the pain, on the other hand, the injury may turn into a much more serious problem and keep you out for the season and perhaps beyond.

The proper treatment for an injury depends on the location of that injury on your body, its severity, and how it occurred. Specific treatments will be covered in the chapters devoted to specific areas of the body, but there are some general steps you should follow in the treatment of *all* sports-related injuries.

First and foremost, pay attention to pain. Pain is your body's way of telling you something is wrong. So if you feel pain in an area, rest it. Next, depending on the severity of your injury, you may need to ice it to decrease the swelling.

In some cases, your injury may necessitate a trip to a medical professional. The following are indications that a trip to the doctor is in order:

➤ Intense pain or tenderness
➤ Pain that increases with activity
➤ Persistent pain
➤ Limping
➤ Numbness
➤ Swelling
➤ Stiffness
➤ Loss of range of motion

Once your injury has been diagnosed, you will go through a series of recovery stages before you can get back on the field or court. In all these stages, you should be closely monitored by your doctor and/or a physical therapist.

During the first stage—the acute stage—if your injury involves swelling, you should try to minimize it with the RICE formula (rest, ice, compression, and elevation), and reduce your activity level. Depending on the type of injury, the acute stage may also involve bracing, casting, or in severe cases, surgery.

It is important that you try to maintain your physical conditioning in the acute stage. If your injury is on your lower body, this may take some creativity, but it is often possible. For instance, if you have a leg injury, you can use a stationary bike or run in water. If one leg is in a cast, you can perform strength-training exercises to stay active.

In the second stage of recovery, you should work to maintain your range of motion in the area of injury. Many muscles will automatically get tight and others will immediately become weak in the setting of an injury, so your doctor or physical therapist will help guide you and provide you with safe range-of-motion exercises.

Once you have regained normal strength and motion in the area, you can begin exercises that continue to improve strength and agility if you have lost any during the rest period. Then, with the approval of your doctor and/or physical therapist, you can start sport-specific movements, possibly with the aid of tape, a brace, or another form of support.

Finally, when you can practice your sport with ease, and your doctor assures you that your likelihood of reinjury is low, you can start to compete again. When you return to competition, you should look out for any warning signs of injury or reinjury, and you should be exceptionally diligent about warming up and cooling down properly.

Depending on the location and severity of your injury, treatment may include the following:

▶ Pain relievers
▶ Anti-inflammatory medications
▶ Physical therapy and/or home exercises
▶ Splint or wrap
▶ Cast

Most sports injuries in teen athletes respond well to nonsurgical treatments. However, in some more severe cases, surgery may be required. The more common sports injuries in teen athletes that require surgery are dislocated shoulders, tears in the anterior cruciate ligament (ACL), and occasionally severe fractures.

Reinjury

According to a study published in the *American Journal of Epidemiology*, high school athletes with a previous injury are two times as likely to injure themselves again. Why? Too many athletes are under pressure to return to play too soon.

In addition to a previous injury, the same study revealed that certain sports—namely, football and soccer—make injury more likely, and that boys are 33 percent more likely than girls to get hurt. It also showed that injuries in high school athletes are more likely to occur during a competition than on the practice field.

So what does all this mean? Be aware of your injury risk factors. The more you realize what puts you at risk for injury, the more you can do for injury prevention. If you have been hurt before, make sure your coach knows this—he or she is likely to be more understanding when you want to pull back due to pain, be it new pain or familiar pain from the old injury.

GETTING BACK IN THE GAME

As soon as you first hear the word *rest,* your number-one question will probably be, "When can I start playing again?" Understandably, you want to get back to the sport you love as soon as possible. But rushing into play too soon may not only extend your time on the bench, it could even do permanent damage and take you out indefinitely. So giving your body adequate time to heal is imperative.

The amount of time necessary to sufficiently rest and heal your injury will depend on your specific situation, and you and your doctor will have to determine a plan of action together. Mild injuries may take you out of only a game or two; moderate injuries may take you out of your sport for three to six weeks or longer; more severe injuries may require surgery and take up to one year (or more in rare cases) to heal. Luckily, in most cases, (and again, depending on the site of your injury), you will be able to stay fit with alternative activities such as swimming, water therapy, rowing, or stationary biking while your injured body part heals.

As you recover, you may need to engage in some sort of rehabilitation (rehab) program, which will also be of help for you to stay in shape and get back to your sport as soon as possible. Rehab may be required as part of your treatment program, or you may decide to engage in it on your own (under the direction of your doctor, of course) to keep your body fit and healthy. Rehab may include manual therapy from a physical therapist, exercise, or technology such as ultrasound, which heats the injured area, speeds healing, and increases your range of motion. No matter what your treatment regimen, the more diligently you follow it, the faster you will return to play.

As a basic rule of thumb, you will be able to return to play when you have regained full range of motion of the injured area without any pain, and you have at least 85 percent full strength. If you suffered a head injury, you will have to be completely symptom-free and back to baseline mental status before you can compete again.

When you finally get the green light from your doctor to return to your sport, you may be tempted to go back to it full-force and play at your preinjury level; after all, you will be eager to get back in the game. It is important that you take it slowly, however. Be sure to warm up adequately before you practice or compete, and take time to cool down when you're done. If you have received any special instructions from your doctor, follow them. And to reduce your risk of reinjury, stop right away if you feel any pain, either in the injured part or any other body part. If any pain persists, tell your doctor.

Also keep in mind that as you ease back into your sport, you may need some new protective gear to help avoid reinjury, including shoes with special inserts or arch supports, tape to wrap and support the injured area, or knee or elbow braces.

TALKING TO YOUR COACH

As a student athlete, your relationship with your coach may be one of the most important and enriching in your life. After all, beyond helping you stay fit and excel in your sport, your coach can teach you a lot about teamwork and dedication, and he or she can act as a mentor for both sport- and nonsport-related issues in your life.

Within your sport, your coach can also provide you with expertise on how to improve your skills, deal with a loss, or psych yourself up before competition. Many coaches have played the sports they coach themselves, so they can offer valuable advice and guidance. Overall, a good relationship with your coach—one based on mutual respect and trust—will be of help to get the most out of your chosen sport.

As with any good relationship, communication will be a crucial part of the relationship with your coach. If you become injured or have a physical limitation that requires certain activity restrictions, an important step in determining when you can get back into the game or how to alter your training schedule will be talking with your coach about your injury and your doctor's treatment plan for you. Most coaches are very understanding and supportive about athletes' injuries, and they respect doctors' orders. However, there are some coaches like Aaron's who pressure students to return to play too soon.

The best way to get your coach's support in the proper healing of your injury or respect of your physical limitation is to keep the lines of communication open. Keep your coach informed throughout the entire course of your injury, from the time it first happens to your diagnosis to your ultimate recovery. The more your coach knows about your injury or condition and your doctor's plans for you, the less likely he or she will be to impart his or her own agenda.

Healing Like a Pro

As a teen athlete, you no doubt pay attention to professional sports. So surely you've noticed that when they are injured, the pros get back on the court or playing field much faster than your average high school quarterback. Why? Professionals are very good at following effective treatment regimens. For that reason, you should take a lesson from the pros.

Professional athletes get prompt treatment as soon as an injury occurs, and this early treatment helps lessen swelling, stiffness, and loss of muscle tone. In addition, professional athletes stay in tip-top shape during their recovery, usually with the help of a personal trainer. And because they love their sports, many professional athletes approach injury with the same positive attitude that they display during competition.

Although you may not have access to many of the resources professional athletes have at their disposal—namely, immediate medical care and 24-hour personal trainers—you can make sure you follow your treatment plan diligently and with a positive attitude. With the right outlook and appropriate amount of rest and cross-training, you will be back out there in no time.

DEALING WITH DIFFERENT TYPES OF COACHES

In general, there are two types of coaches—those who lead based on responsibility, and those who lead based on obedience—and understanding the category your particular coach fits into will help you best deal with him or her.

Responsibility coaches, as their name suggests, put more responsibility on student athletes, and they give them more say in the way the team is run. For instance, if a team member is chronically late, a responsibility coach might ask other team members how to handle the situation. A responsibility coach might also ask athletes for suggestions on new stretches to add to the warm-up routine. In general, a responsibility coach runs his or her team in a more relaxed, laid-back way, and it will probably be easier to maintain open communication with this type of coach, particularly in the face of an injury.

Obedience coaches, on the other hand, run their teams with themselves in charge. They make the rules, and they expect their athletes to follow them. To develop a productive, working relationship with an obedience coach, you will have to show him or her a great deal of respect and demonstrate that you have confidence in his or her skills and authority. If you get injured, an obedience coach will still want to do things his or her way, whether that means respecting your doctor's orders or urging you to play through pain.

You should approach both types of coaches—responsibility coaches and obedience coaches—with a similar level of respect and openness. Both styles of coaches will respond best if you work hard, listen to their advice, and approach them with problems—injuries included—as soon as they arise.

Keep in mind that no matter what kind of coach you have, you may—regularly or occasionally—bump heads with him or her. The nature of the coach/athlete relationship sometimes leads to disagreements over the amount of playtime or favoritism toward or bias against certain players. Some coaches focus on winning at the expense of striving to improve, which makes athletes feel pressured to win and underappreciated when they show personal improvements despite losing on the field or court.

If at any point during the course of your injury you don't agree with your coach's treatment or guidance, talk to him or her about it right away. Request that you and your coach set a time to sit down and talk. (Trying to talk to a coach when he or she is in the middle of a game or rushing before practice won't yield the best results.) Once you have the coach alone, clearly ask about the reasons behind the plans for you. Keep in mind that your coach may not have realized the severity of your injury or condition or your doctor's insistence that you take a break. If this is the case, reiterate this information clearly and be ready to present any documentation from your doctor.

If after talking with your coach you feel that you are still not being heard, or if you are hesitant to talk with him or her about an injury or physical limitation (or any other problem you are having, for that matter), consider talking to your team captain first. One of the team captain's jobs is to act as a middleman between athletes and the coach.

If all else fails and your coach continues to drive you to the point that you fear you will worsen an existing injury, reinjure a past injury, or put yourself in danger of any sort, tell your parents what is going on; they will be able to set up a meeting with the coach's supervisor—your school's principal or athletic director. Or discuss these concerns with your physician—he or she can get involved if necessary.

Once you've healed, look to your coach for advice on how to avoid a subsequent injury. Most coaches have been trained in how to prevent injuries, and they can guide you on how to stay healthy and injury-free by way of proper warm-up, and supportive measures such as bandages, tape, and wraps.

THE PRE-PARTICIPATION EXAM

To make sure you are physically fit enough to participate in a sport, your physician will conduct a pre-participation exam or "sports physical" before you start the season. This examination is meant to point out your strengths and weaknesses, and to identify any conditions that might make playing a sport unsafe for you. In all but one of the 50 states—Rhode Island—a pre-participation exam is required before a student can play a school sport.

The pre-participation sports exam (PPE) is not meant to be a comprehensive physical exam, but instead it is meant to do the following:

> ▸ Identify any life-threatening conditions that could lead to complications during sports participation. Medical conditions that may present problems in young athletes include cardiovascular conditions, such as
> - Hypertrophic cardiomyopathy (HCM)
> - Coronary artery anomalies
> - Myocarditis
> - Aortic rupture (Marfan syndrome)

> ‣ Identify any conditions that should be treated before sports participation. Conditions that require treatment before exercise include
>   - Exercise-induced bronchoconstriction (EIB)
>   - High blood pressure
>   - Eating disorders, such as anorexia or bulimia
>   - Diabetes
>   - Musculoskelatal problems (i.e., hamstring tightness and ankle weakness)

> ‣ Remove any unnecessary previous restrictions on sports participation. Some conditions lead physicians to restrict teenagers' participation in sports; however, when managed appropriately, these conditions can safely coexist with sports activities. Examples of these conditions include *Osgood-Schlatter disease* and obesity.
> ‣ Diagnose any old injuries and treat them accordingly. Previous injury is the strongest predictor of future sports injury.
> ‣ Provide suggestions as to how athletes can prevent injuries and perhaps even optimize performance.

The PPE usually takes place four to six weeks before the sports season, so doctors have enough time to diagnose and treat any relevant musculoskeletal injuries or conditions. Depending on your school, one doctor may conduct the entire examination, or you may go through a series of stations specific to certain areas of your body. You may also go to your family physician for your PPE, or have it done on-site at your school.

The PPE consists of the following components:

> ‣ Your medical history, including a history of your general medical health, cardiovascular history, and family history of certain diseases and conditions. The doctor performing the exam will pay particular attention to any current conditions you have, prior surgeries, loss of organ function, current medications you are taking, any history of heat-related illness, your immunization (shot) history, menstrual history if you are female, and any history of rapid weight loss or gain.
> ‣ Your injury history, including past injuries, loss of consciousness after a past head injury, or previous exclusion from sports for any reason.
> ‣ Your cardiovascular history, including any history of high blood pressure, heart murmur, heart palpitations, dizziness or

Sample Letter to Draft with Your Doctor Documenting Your Injury

Here is a sample of a brief letter you can draft with your doctor to document your diagnosed injury or physical limitation and the playing restrictions that accompany it. Present this letter to your coach as soon as you receive your diagnosis and instructions for rehabilitation.

Dear [COACH'S NAME],

[YOUR NAME] is under my care for [NAME OF DIAGNOSED INJURY]. For the safety and well-being of [YOUR NAME], and to assure that [YOUR NAME] returns to the playing field in the fastest and safest manner possible, I am providing information and instructions regarding [YOUR NAME]'s participation in physical activities.

[ASK YOUR DOCTOR TO DESCRIBE THE NATURE OF YOUR INJURY.]

Sincerely,
[DOCTOR'S NAME]

For example, here is a sample letter for a student athlete with exercise-induced asthma:

Dear [COACH'S NAME],

[YOUR NAME] can engage in regular physical activities most of the time. However, activities may need to be curtailed during asthma episodes.

Because every student with exercise-induced asthma has a different level of tolerance, please allow [YOUR NAME] to exercise at [YOUR NAME]'s own pace. Teenagers with exercise-induced asthma sometimes have difficulty running laps, particularly when the weather is cold. Please do not force [YOUR NAME] to exercise beyond [YOUR NAME]'s comfort level.

(continues)

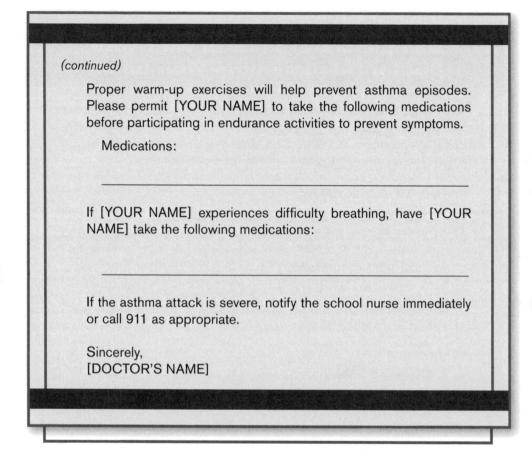

(continued)

Proper warm-up exercises will help prevent asthma episodes. Please permit [YOUR NAME] to take the following medications before participating in endurance activities to prevent symptoms.

Medications:

_____

If [YOUR NAME] experiences difficulty breathing, have [YOUR NAME] take the following medications:

_____

If the asthma attack is severe, notify the school nurse immediately or call 911 as appropriate.

Sincerely,
[DOCTOR'S NAME]

shortness of breath during exercise, chest pain, or family history of cardiovascular disease.

> A musculoskeletal exam, including tests for flexibility and strength, and a review of any previous injuries.
> A check of your blood pressure, heart rate, and heart rhythms.
> An eye exam.
> Screening for conditions that may restrict sports participation. These conditions include scoliosis, elbow dislocation, knee instability, femur fracture, single testicle in males, recurrent concussion, abdominal mass, or heart arrhythmia.
> Detection of any other medical conditions that may restrict participation in your chosen sport.

At the end of the PPE, your doctor will give you full clearance to participate in your sport, clearance to participate with limitations, or exclusion from participation until further evaluation. The doctor may also order follow-up tests or make recommendations for the athlete to follow prior to or during participation. If the doctor places any restrictions on your participation, he or she will discuss these with you clearly and give you a plan for treatment or limitations.

WHAT YOU NEED TO KNOW

> Injuries are quite prevalent among high school athletes; each year, approximately 30 million students participate in organized sports in the United States, and an estimated 20 percent experience sports-related musculoskeletal injuries.

> Sports injuries come in many forms, but they fall into two general categories—overuse injuries and acute injuries. Overuse injuries occur when muscles, tendons, growth plates, or bones cannot keep up with the stress put on them, so they break down and cause pain.

> Proper conditioning, which includes stretching, endurance training, and strength training, helps prevent sports injuries in teens.

> Other methods to help prevent sports injuries include warming up, cooling down, making sure you are adequately hydrated, cross-training, and using proper safety equipment that fits properly.

> No matter how a sports injury occurred or where on your body it took place, it's important that you start to take care of it as soon as possible, preferably in the first two days or so.

> The following are indications that a trip to the doctor is in order: intense pain or tenderness; pain that increases with activity; persistent pain; limping; numbness; swelling; stiffness; loss of range of motion.

> When you return to competition, you should look out for any warning signs of injury or reinjury, and you should be exceptionally diligent about warming up and cooling down properly.

> As a basic rule of thumb, you will be able to return to play when you have regained full range of motion of the injured area without any pain, and you have at least 85 percent full strength.

> The best way to get your coach's support in the proper healing of your injury or respect of your physical limitation is to keep the lines of communication open.

2

From Concussions to Ankle Sprains: Types of Sports Injuries

Jenna, 16, twisted her ankle during her last high school tennis match. It swelled immediately, and now—a day later—it is black and blue. Jenna's ankle is causing her a lot of pain, but she's hesitant to see her doctor for the injury, because she's not sure if it is serious enough to require treatment. Plus, she doesn't want to find out that she has to take a break from playing tennis at the peak of her competitive season.

Jenna is wrong about not seeing her doctor. The pain, swelling, and discoloration are all indications that she needs treatment. If she ignores the injury, it will only worsen and could take her away from tennis not only for a few days or weeks, but for the entire season or longer.

Sports injuries like Jenna's come in many forms and severities. Jenna could have experienced only a mild *sprain* or *strain*—an injury that may heal rather quickly—or she may have suffered a more severe sprain or *fracture*, which will take her off the tennis court for much longer.

This chapter will explain the different kinds of injuries that teens may suffer while playing sports—muscle injuries, tendon injuries, ligament injuries, fractures, and more—as well as the sports and activities that can cause or exacerbate these injuries. It will also present readers with some of the rules doctors use when diagnosing injuries, so teens like Jenna will know whether or not they should see a doctor.

The many different middle and high school sports may involve many different types of sports injuries that can occur in teens. Sports activities can result in injuries that range from post-workout soreness, minor bruises and aches that you can play through, to serious injuries to muscles, tendons, ligaments, bones, and joints that can take you out of your sport for the whole season or longer. These injuries can occur in teens for a variety of reasons, including lack of appropriate safety equipment or footwear, improper training, and fast growth during puberty.

The areas of your body most at risk for injuries depend on the particular sport you play. Although your back, arms, and legs are most at-risk for injury, sports injuries can occur anywhere on the body—your face, neck, sex organs, hands, head, and feet.

The most common types of sports injuries in young people are overuse injuries and acute injuries, and these injuries can occur in the form of fractures, ligament sprains or tears, tendon/muscle injuries, concussions, eye injuries, and spinal cord injuries.

OVERUSE INJURIES

About half of the injuries that occur in middle and high school athletes are overuse injuries. These days, more teenagers than ever are participating in the same sport year round or training too intensely, therefore causing their bodies to break down in the form of overuse injuries.

Overuse injuries or chronic injuries occur over a period of time and result from sports that involve prolonged, repetitive motions or impacts such as baseball, basketball, running, tennis, bowling, gymnastics, and swimming. Examples of repetitive motions that tend to result in overuse injuries are running, underhand throwing, or serving a ball in tennis. They range from *tendonitis,* chronic muscle strains, and ligament strains to stress fractures.

Sports that involve repetitive arm motions, such as swimming, tennis, and baseball, often lead to overuse injuries in the shoulder and elbow; sports that require gripping, such as gymnastics, golf, bowling, and tennis, more commonly result in overuse injuries in the forearm and hand, sports that involve repetitive motions in the leg, such as running, jumping, or basketball, result in more injuries to the hip, thigh, knee, leg, or ankle/foot.

Overuse injuries also tend more commonly to occur in teen athletes who are improperly trained or conditioned. For instance, a football player may show up to fall practices after taking the entire summer off from exercise, only to find himself hobbling on an injury a few weeks later. These types of overuse injuries are particularly prevalent in cheerleaders, who often do not train as rigorously as competitive athletes.

Overuse injuries can also result from insufficient rest after an injury, either because an athlete refuses to stop training or because his or her coach encourages him or her to play through pain. Overuse injuries include the following:

Stress fractures. Stress fractures are tiny cracks or weak spots that appear on the surface of a bone when excessive, prolonged, repetitive stress is placed on the bone. They are common in athletes who perform high-impact activities such as running, and they occur most often in the legs and feet. Your muscles usually absorb some of the shock when you move, but over time, these muscles grow tired and can't absorb as much impact. For instance, a basketball player who continuously jumps on the court may develop a stress fracture in his or her leg.

Growth-related overuse injuries. Also called apophysitis, one type of stress injury that is particularly prevalent in young athletes is to the growth areas of the long bones in the arms and legs, and occasionally the hands and feet. During times of more rapid growth, the bones increase in length at a faster rate than the tendons and ligaments, making the attachment sites more vulnerable to injury. Repetitive stresses to these areas may cause injury, resulting in pain, swelling, and impaired performance. One common example is called Osgood-Schlatter disease, found just below the knee. Most of these injuries are not serious, and they are treated with rest/activity modification until the young athlete is feeling better, in addition to proper stretching and strengthening.

Tendonitis. Tendonitis is the irritation, inflammation, and swelling of a tendon that results from repetitive stretching/straining. Tendons are fibrous materials that attach muscle to bone, and they can vary in size from the large tendons around your knee joint to the tiny tendons in your fingers.

Ligament strain. Often referred to as a "pull," a ligament strain is the stretching or tearing of a ligament, for example, a pulled hamstring or back.

Treatment of overuse injuries. Although teens with overuse injuries like Jenna may be tempted to ignore them, these injuries can be just as severe as acute injuries, and they should be treated as such.

Remember: Just because an injury doesn't occur in a sudden, dramatic fashion doesn't mean it will heal on its own. If a chronic injury goes untreated, it will probably get worse over time and necessitate more treatment than it would have if it were caught early on.

It is also important to note that some overuse injuries such as stress fractures and tendonitis may not show up on X-rays; so in some cases, a doctor will diagnose them based on symptoms alone.

Treatment for overuse injuries usually includes "RICE," crutches, cast immobilization, and physical therapy. RICE stands for:

▸ **Rest** helps small blood vessels to seal and, therefore, stop bleeding.
▸ **Ice** the injury. Icing the injured area helps constrict blood vessels. When blood vessels constrict, it limits bleeding to the area and, therefore, helps reduce swelling.
▸ Use **Compression**. Compressing an injured area with an elastic bandage or wrap restricts the space into which blood can flow, reducing swelling.
▸ **Elevate** the injured body part as often as you can. Elevating the injury above your heart increases the ability of the swelling to drain.

In addition to helping to speed healing of a current injury, RICE also helps prevent future injury. For example: Icing an injury will help stop the bleeding and, therefore, prevent calcium deposits from forming later on. Elevation forces the injured person to take weight off the injured part, thus preventing further damage.

ACUTE INJURIES

Acute sports injuries usually result from a sudden trauma. For instance, they may occur after a twisted ankle on the soccer field, a fall during a football game, or a collision with another player on the basketball court. Acute sports injuries in teens commonly include *bruises* (also called contusions), *abrasions, lacerations,* strains (partial or complete tears of muscles or tendons), sprains (partial or complete ligament tears), and fractures.

Bruise. Caused by a direct blow, a bruise is swelling or bleeding in a muscle or other soft body tissue.

Abrasion. An abrasion, or scrape, is any injury that rubs off the surface of the skin.

Laceration. A laceration is an irregular tearlike wound due to some form of blunt trauma (i.e., when skin splits open on face during boxing).

Strain. Not to be confused with a sprain, an acute strain is an injury to a muscle or tendon. Muscles are tissues made of bundles of cells that contract and produce movement when stimulated by nerves. Tendons are fibrous materials that attach muscle to bone, and they can vary in size from the large tendons around your knee joint to the tiny tendons in your fingers. Strains can occur on any part of the body where there is muscle. Examples of strains include pulled hamstrings and groins. Strains often occur when there is an excessive load placed on a muscle (i.e., lifting a weight that is too heavy) or a sudden stretch of the muscle (attempting to sprint before warming up). Staying in shape and keeping athletic activities within your fitness level can usually prevent strains. These range from mild injuries to more severe muscle or tendon tears.

Sprain. A sprain is an acute injury to the ligaments surrounding a joint, such as the ankle or wrist. Ligaments are the bands of tough, fibrous tissue that connect two or more bones at a joint. Sprains can result from awkward falls or landings during play that force a joint past its usual range of motion. Ankle sprains are the most common sports-related injuries in the United States.

Fracture. A fracture is a crack or break in a bone. Fractures usually occur as a result of some kind of impact such as a fall or a hit or kick from an opponent.

Concussion. A concussion is a violent jarring or shock to the head that causes a temporary jolt to the brain, usually resulting from a blow to the head or a fall. Symptoms of a concussion include confusion, loss of consciousness, and short-term memory problems. A severe concussion can lead to a hematoma—bleeding or pooling of blood inside the brain—or in rare cases, brain damage.

Muscle pull or tear. A muscle pull occurs when a muscle and its fibers stretch beyond their capacity, usually as a result of a sudden, severe force. If most of the muscle fibers are pulled and only a few are torn, the injury is still classified as a muscle "pull." If many of the fibers have been torn, it is a muscle "tear."

Muscle spasm. Some people who fear they have a torn muscle are actually experiencing a *muscle spasm*—tightness in the muscle that results from intense exercise. In fact, some injuries that are initially diagnosed as muscle pulls turn out to be low-grade muscle spasms.

Trauma to organs in the abdomen or chest. In some sports, there is the potential for injuries to organs in the abdomen and chest area, such as the spleen, liver, and lungs. The most commonly injured organ during sports is the spleen. Although rare, these types of injuries tend to occur in contact sports such as football or lacrosse (after a particularly hard hit or tackle) or baseball (when a player is hit with a ball).

Treatment of acute injuries. To manage acute sports injuries until they can be evaluated by a medical professional, in most cases, experts also recommend RICE, described above.

HEAT-RELATED ILLNESSES

Not all sports-related conditions are injuries per se. One condition that occurs fairly often in teenage athletes, particularly in warm weather, is heat-related illness. Heat-related illnesses are always dangerous and can potentially be fatal, so they should not be ignored. They are a particular threat to children and teenagers because children and teenagers perspire less than adults and, therefore, require a higher core body temperature to start sweating. Heat-related illness falls into the following categories:

Dehydration. *Dehydration* is a deficit in body fluids. It can be caused by vomiting, diarrhea, or in the case of sports, excessive sweating due to heat and/or exertion. Symptoms include dry, sticky mouth, tiredness, thirst, decreased urine output, muscle weakness, headache, and dizziness or light-headedness.

Hyponatremia. The opposite of dehydration, *hyponatremia* occurs when the sodium in your blood becomes diluted from drinking too much water. It tends to occur in novice endurance athletes with long finishing times. Hyponatremia can be acute, occurring suddenly, or chronic, building over a few weeks. Hyponatremia can lead to rapid brain swelling, coma, or even death, so it must be treated immediately. Symptoms include nausea and vomiting, confusion, headache, loss of appetite, fatigue, restlessness, irritability, muscle weakness, muscle spasms, muscle cramps, and loss of consciousness.

Heat exhaustion. *Heat exhaustion* is a potentially serious condition that results from prolonged exposure to high temperatures. Symptoms include nausea, dizziness, weakness, headache, heavy perspiration, pale and moist skin, dilated pupils, low body temperature, weak pulse, fainting, and disorientation.

Heat stroke. *Heat stroke,* one of the leading causes of death on the football field, is a medical emergency that results when the body's internal thermostat fails to keep the body cool, causing body temperature to rise up to 108 degrees Fahrenheit. Symptoms include hot and dry skin, a cease in sweating, and loss of consciousness. A teen athlete who experiences these symptoms should be immersed in ice and sent to the emergency room immediately.

WHEN TO SEE A DOCTOR

Like your own personal bodyguard, pain is nature's way of telling you that something is wrong. Take a minute to think about what it would be like if you didn't feel pain: Instead of pulling your hand away from a hot stove, you'd leave it there while your skin burned. Rather than taking the weight off a fractured foot, you'd walk on it, worsening the break. You feel pain for a reason, and you should heed its warning.

However, pain—and the injuries that cause it—varies widely from mild to severe. (This is why health-care professionals developed the pain scale of 1 to 10). Treatments for these injuries vary from minor cuts and scrapes to medical emergencies. Young athletes experience little bumps, bruises, and other minor injuries on the playing field every day. After applying a Band-Aid and a little antiseptic ointment on the sidelines, they are good to go again. On the other hand, if an athlete is unconscious or unable to walk, clearly a trip to the doctor or emergency room is in order.

There are a few injuries that require immediate medical attention, including the following:

Fractures. Fractures, or breaks or cracks in a bone, may result from acute or overuse injuries; either way, they necessitate treatment. Fractures range in severity from tiny hairline cracks to compound fractures that break through the skin.

Concussions. If you or one of your team members experiences any symptoms of a concussion—loss of short-term memory, loss of consciousness, or confusion—after a blow to the head, medical attention is in order.

Severe ligament or cartilage injuries. Serious injuries to ligaments or *cartilage*, such as an injury to the *anterior cruciate ligament* (ACL) of the knee, require immediate treatment. If the damage is not repaired quickly, these injuries can recur or cause arthritis in the future.

Spine injuries. Any injury to the back that appears to involve the spine should be checked out by a medical professional immediately. In the meantime, the athlete should lie still.

Some injuries are somewhere in the middle of minor and severe, in a gray area that leaves athletes and their parents and coaches confused about whether they should seek medical care. Ultimately, the decision to head to the doctor or emergency room is up to you and your parents.

When you experience specific symptoms. As a rule of thumb, if any of the following symptoms accompany an injury, you should seek medical attention:

- You have intense pain that increases with activity.
- Your pain is persistent.
- You have pain that increases when you press on a bone. This may indicate a fracture and should be evaluated with an X-ray.
- You are experiencing swelling. Any swelling should be evaluated with an X-ray to rule out a fracture.
- You are limping.
- You cannot put weight on the area.
- You have numbness or tingling.
- You are experiencing weakness in the area.
- The injured area is stiff.
- The injured area is severely discolored.
- You have a decreased range of motion.
- You experience little or no improvement after 48 to 72 hours of RICE.

If you are having trouble making the decision of whether or not to seek medical attention for an injury, talk to a trainer. Most high schools have certified athletic trainers on staff and present at sporting competitions. These trainers are specially versed in the initial management and triage of acute sports injuries, including giving advice on whether or not to seek medical care. Too often, teen athletes refrain from seeking attention for a potential injury because they are afraid of being pulled from the competition. But this kind of thinking will only delay your return to play if you are indeed injured.

You should also learn to recognize the difference between normal soreness and chronic pain, which can signal an existing or impending injury. Soreness is your body's normal response to pushing itself. If you are a runner, you may experience soreness after a particularly intense cross-country race or track meet, and if you play football, you may be sore after a rough game. Called *delayed onset muscle soreness* (DOMS), this soreness usually sets in 24 to 72 hours after strenuous exercise, and it is temporary, subsiding within two to three days. Chronic pain, on the other hand, persists. See your doctor if pain lingers for a week or more, or if the pain progresses from happening only after you've finished exercising to showing up while you're participating in daily activities.

Another pain-causing condition that can occur in teen athletes is *rhabdomyolysis,* a breakdown of muscle fibers into the bloodstream that can lead to kidney damage. In the case of exercise, rhabdomyolysis results from an overuse of muscles or a trauma to a muscle and causes symptoms such as weakness, muscle stiffness or aching, muscle tenderness, and muscle weakness. Because it can lead to kidney damage, rhabdomyolysis should be treated right away. The most common treatment is rehydration with fluids, either by drinking them or in more severe cases, taking them in through an I.V.

Once you've determined that your pain warrants treatment, first, stop doing whatever activity or sport caused the injury and make an appointment to see your doctor. If your injury is severe, head to the emergency room.

WHAT TO DO WHEN AN INJURY OCCURS

Immediately after an injury occurs, be sure to take your time getting off the field or court. Although you may feel pressure from your teammates, the coach, and spectators to rush off the field so the team can get on with the competition, don't move until you feel it is safe. This is particularly important if there is a chance you've suffered an injury to your neck or spinal cord. And if you are not sure if you can walk off the field, don't take a chance—wait for a stretcher.

Use RICE: rest, ice, compression, elevation. You will hear this acronym repeatedly throughout the book. Use RICE immediately following an acute injury or to ease the pain of an overuse injury until you can be seen by a doctor. RICE will help to reduce swelling and prevent further damage.

Note how the injury happened. Because swelling and pain often mask the true source of an injury, it will be helpful if you, your coach, or one of your teammates can inform the doctor about how the injury occurred. If the doctor knows where you were hit, how you fell, and what you were doing at the time of the injury, he or she can make a more accurate diagnosis.

Take over-the-counter (OTC) pain relievers as needed. While you're waiting to see the doctor, you can take an OTC painkiller such as aspirin, ibuprofen, or acetaminophen in most cases. Both aspirin and ibuprofen (Advil, Motrin) reduce pain and inflammation. Acetaminophen (Tylenol) just helps to relieve pain but is less irritating to the stomach than aspirin or ibuprofen. As a side note, never take aspirin with another anti-inflammatory medication, as it could lead to a toxic reaction. Also, never mix acetaminophen with alcoholic beverages, because the combination could cause serious liver damage.

If your injury turns out to be complicated, you may be referred to a health-care professional who specializes in orthopedics or sports medicine.

WHAT TO EXPECT AT THE DOCTOR

Once you get in to see a health-care professional—whether you make an appointment or head to the emergency room—he or she will examine your injury and may use tools such as *magnetic resonance imaging* (MRI), an X-ray, or a CT scan to determine the extent of the problem. If your health-care professional suspects you have a soft tissue injury, such as an injury to a ligament, tendon, cartilage, nerve, or muscle, he or she will often perform an MRI, as it will provide a clearer picture of soft tissue. The physician may also order an MRI to rule out a stress fracture in the event that a fracture didn't show up on an X-ray.

After the doctor has determined the extent of your injury, he or she will probably start with conservative treatments, such as RICE, to help decrease the initial swelling. He or she may also prescribe an anti-inflammatory medication, such as naproxen sodium (Aleve) or ibuprofen (Advil, Motrin), or instruct you to take one of these medications over-the-counter. Depending on the severity of your injury, the doctor may also prescribe a splint, brace, cast, or in extreme cases, surgery.

From there, the doctor may recommend that you refrain from playing your sport while you heal; give you the green light to play, but only if you use a protective device such as a wrist or knee brace/guard; or order you to undergo physical therapy/rehabilitation. If your doctor thinks you are at risk for worsening the current injury or aggravating a previous injury, he or she will not allow you to play your sport.

What's Best for an Injury— Heat or Ice?

The answer is, it depends on your injury. If you have just suffered an acute injury to a bone, muscle, or joint, you should use ice. If you have a chronic, nagging muscle injury, on the other hand, heat should be your treatment of choice. In general, ice is a good idea for the first two to three days following an injury.

When it comes to treating an acute injury, ice will reduce pain and swelling. Real ice wrapped in a plastic bag or towel is better than a chemical cold pack. "Burping" the bag (letting the air out before sealing it) often helps to make it more moldable around the injured site. You should apply the ice pack directly to the site of your injury, wrap it in place with mild compression, and elevate the area of your injury above your heart if possible. This process is described with the acronym RICE (rest, ice, compression, and elevation). Ice the area for 20 to 30 minutes, then repeat the RICE process once the skin has returned to its normal temperature. If there is some sort of a barrier between the ice and the injury site, such as a bandage or wrap, extend the treatment time a few minutes.

In the case of a chronic condition such as a muscle strain, heat will help relax and loosen tissues and stimulate blood flow to the area to speed healing. Use a heating pad or hot, wet towel as the source of your heat and apply it for no more than 20 minutes at a time. The best time to heat an injury is before activity to loosen tissues and relax the injured area.

And thus begins the road to recovery. Depending on the extent of your injury, this road may be long or short. But if you want to return to play healthy and in tip-top shape, it is not a road you can sidestep. This book will help pave the way.

WHAT YOU NEED TO KNOW

▶ About half of the injuries that occur in middle and high school athletes are overuse injuries. Overuse injuries (also known as

What Happens When a Teen Breaks a Growth Plate?

Not all fractures are created equal. A fracture in an adult is different from a fracture in a child or teenager. If a fracture in a child or teen involves the end of a bone, a growth plate—an area of the bone crucial to the bone's growth—may be affected. About half of all *growth plate injuries* in teenagers occur in the wrist, specifically in the outer bone of the forearm (radius). Growth plate injures are also fairly common in the lower bones of the leg, the tibia and fibula, the femur in the thigh, and in the hip, foot, and ankle bones.

The good news about growth plate injuries is that they rarely cause long-term problems. However, if left alone, some growth plate injuries may result in a bone that is shorter or more angled than normal, so treatment is in order.

If a fracture is in a location where a growth plate might be involved, your physician will order an X-ray. Occasionally, an X-ray will not show a fracture even though one has occurred. So in some cases, if a child or teenager experiences pain over the area of a growth plate or bone, the doctor will treat for a growth plate injury just in case there is such a fracture. If an X-ray *does* indicate a growth plate injury, treatment will involve alignment if the fracture is displaced, and a case, splint, or other form of immobilization. If alignment is necessary, it will usually be done under sedation. If the fracture is severe enough, surgery may be required, along with fixation with pins, plates, or screws. Throughout the process, the physician will probably continue to use X-rays as a means to follow the healing of the fracture.

chronic injuries) occur over a period of time and result from sports that include prolonged, repetitive motions or impacts, such as baseball, basketball, running, tennis, bowling, gymnastics, and swimming.

▶ Overuse injuries can also occur in teen athletes who are improperly trained or conditioned, and they can result from insufficient rest after an injury, either because an athlete refuses to stop training or because his or her coach encourages him or her to play through pain.

▶ Although teens with overuse injuries may be tempted to ignore them, these injuries can be just as severe as acute injuries and, therefore, they should be treated as such.

▶ Acute sports injuries in teens usually result from a sudden trauma and commonly include bruises (also called contusions), abrasions, lacerations, strains (partial or complete tears of muscles or tendons), sprains (partial or complete ligament tears), and fractures.

▶ To manage acute sports injuries until a medical professional can evaluate them, experts also recommend RICE, described above.

▶ Heat-related illnesses are always dangerous and potentially can be fatal.

▶ Like your own personal bodyguard, pain is nature's way of telling you that something is wrong.

▶ As a rule of thumb, if any of the following symptoms accompany an injury, you should seek medical care:

• You have intense pain that increases with activity.
• Your pain is persistent.
• You have pain that increases when you press on a bone. This may indicate a fracture and should be evaluated with an X-ray.
• You are experiencing swelling. Any swelling should be evaluated with an X-ray to rule out a fracture.
• You are limping.
• You cannot put weight on the area.
• You have numbness or tingling.
• You are experiencing weakness in the injured area.
• The injured area is stiff.
• The injured area is severely discolored.
• You have a decreased range of motion.
• You experience little or no improvement after 48 to 72 hours of RICE.

▶ Immediately following an acute injury, take your time getting off the field or court, use RICE, note how the injury happened, and take an over-the-counter painkiller such as ibuprofen or acetaminophen.

Head and Neck Injuries

Brian, 17, is the star quarterback on his high school football team. During his last game against their rival team, Brian fell hard during a tackle. He was unconscious for a few seconds, and his head hurt immediately afterward, but he quickly started to feel better, so he decided to rejoin the game about 30 minutes later.

This was a big mistake. Only a few minutes after returning to the game, Brian was hit again. Although the blow wasn't as hard as the first one, it knocked Brian out completely. The first blow had caused a mild concussion and, therefore, swelling in Brian's brain. Then, when he was hit the second time, his already bruised brain suffered even more damage, sending Brian to the hospital and out of play for more than a month.

It's not surprising that Brian didn't realize he had a concussion; some surveys have found that more than 80 percent of people with concussions don't recognize them as such. But the fact that Brian was unconscious should have alerted him and his coach that an immediate trip to the hospital was in order. Head and neck injuries are potentially very serious and should not be taken lightly.

Head and neck injuries are some of the most serious injuries suffered by high school athletes, yet they are also among the most common. You can injure your head or neck through a sudden dramatic injury during contact sports such as football or rugby, or sports that have the potential for falling accidents, such as horseback riding or gymnastics.

This chapter will cover some of the most common injuries of the head and neck and offer advice on how teen athletes can best prevent and treat these injuries. Some of the specific injuries covered will include stingers and *burners,* fractures, strains, sprains, whiplash, and concussions.

Head injuries can occur in any high school sport, but they are particularly common in field hockey, football, gymnastics, ice hockey, lacrosse, martial arts, soccer, boxing, and wrestling.

Since your head houses your brain and, therefore, all your body's central control centers, any injury to the head that appears to be more severe than a mild bump or scrape should be seen by a doctor. You simply cannot be too cautious when it comes to head injuries.

CONCUSSION

A concussion (also called a mild traumatic brain injury) is any loss of consciousness or disorientation after a blow to the head. According to the Centers for Disease Control and Prevention (CDC), 20 percent of concussions—or 300,000 concussions per year—result from football injuries. Males are more at risk for concussions than females, and about half of people who suffer concussions are between the ages of 15 and 34.

There are many degrees of concussion, and there are multiple guidelines for "grading" concussions. In the case of a mild concussion, you may be stunned/dazed for a few seconds and may have some trouble remembering what you are doing or how the injury occurred. If the concussion is severe, you may be unconscious for several minutes. Other symptoms of a concussion include the following:

- Inability to remember what happened right before or after the injury (amnesia)
- Confusion
- Asking the same questions repeatedly
- Dizziness
- Light-headedness
- Blurred vision
- Double vision
- Sensitivity to light and noise
- Problems sleeping
- Ringing in the ears (tinnitus)

Physically, someone with a concussion may have a vacant stare or a confused facial expression, be slower to answer questions or follow instructions than normal, be easily distracted, be disoriented, and have slurred speech. He or she may also not make sense when talking or appear uncoordinated.

Concussion symptoms usually show up in the first 24 hours after the injury, especially in the case of a more severe concussion, and they can persist for days, weeks, or months.

Treatment of a concussion involves rest to protect against further head injury. Even if you immediately regain consciousness (as in Brian's case, mentioned earlier), you should see a doctor. You should also be watched carefully for danger signs of possible bleeding inside the head, such as headache, nausea, and further loss of consciousness. Whether or not you look and feel fine after the injury, you should be monitored for at least 24 hours for any of these signs.

If you are unconscious for an extended period of time (more than a few seconds) or you do not recover from the blow to your head immediately, emergency medical care is in order. At the hospital, you will undergo a neurological examination. Typically, this exam involves a check of your muscle strength, balance, reflexes, and the pressure in the back of your eyes. In some cases, the physician may also look at your brain with a CT scan or MRI, although these tests usually only show an abnormality if the concussion is severe.

Once you return home, your caregiver should look out for the following warning signs. If you exhibit any of these symptoms, you or your caregiver should seek medical attention right away:

> ➤ A severe or worsening headache
> ➤ Inability to be awakened or aroused
> ➤ Restlessness, unsteadiness, or seizures
> ➤ Confusion
> ➤ Vision problems
> ➤ Fever
> ➤ Vomiting
> ➤ Stiff neck
> ➤ Problems with urine or bowel control
> ➤ Weakness or numbness in any part of the body

Grade One, Two, and Three Concussions. To distinguish their severity, concussions are often put into "grade" categories, per guidelines for concussion grading set by the American Academy of Neurology (AAN).

In the case of a grade one (or mild) concussion, the athlete does not lose consciousness, but he or she may have trouble remembering events for up to 15 minutes after the injury took place. This type of concussion makes up 90 percent of concussions suffered by teen athletes, and it may unfortunately often be overlooked by both athlete and coach. In most cases, however, even a grade one concussion will cause an athlete to leave the competition.

With a grade two (moderate) concussion, the athlete also does not lose consciousness, but he or she may be confused and experience mental status changes that last longer than 15 minutes after the injury.

Grade three (severe) concussions consist of a period of unconsciousness that is either brief, lasting for seconds, or prolonged, lasting for minutes.

Grade two and three concussions are much more obvious and, therefore, usually easily recognized by coaches.

Return to Play. When you suffer a concussion, your brain swells, and even a small subsequent hit could cause severe brain damage. So you must be extremely careful when it comes to returning to play. There have been reported cases of teenagers who have died after returning to play too soon after a seemingly mild head injury.

This phenomenon, also known as "second impact syndrome," occurs when a second concussion takes place while an athlete is still healing from a previous concussion. Because the brain is already injured and swelled, the second impact is more likely to cause widespread damage, possibly even death, and the athlete doesn't even have to lose consciousness for this damage to occur. After an athlete suffers a first concussion, his or her risk for sustaining a second one is dramatically increased. Repeat concussions, even when they are mild, increase the chances of post-concussion side effects (discussed below) as well.

So until a concussion has been ruled out or healed completely, you should sit safely on the bench. If it's been determined that you have suffered a mild, grade one concussion, most guidelines will permit you to return to play if your symptoms are minor, and resolve quickly, and you have had no loss of consciousness.

Because you cannot see the extent of injury with a concussion, it can be difficult to know when you are OK to return to play. Therefore, there are no hard-and-fast rules about when you can get back out there. No matter what, you shouldn't return to play before you have gotten the green light from your physician. As a general rule of thumb, most physicians and trainers follow these AAN guidelines:

> ▸ If it is your first concussion and it is a grade one concussion, stop competing immediately and rest on the sidelines. If after

15 minutes, your physician/trainer determines that you are OK and you no longer have symptoms, you can return to play.

➤ If it is your first concussion and it is a grade two concussion, stop competing immediately and rest on the sidelines. Do not return to play until you are symptom-free for seven consecutive days.

➤ If it is a first concussion and it is a grade three concussion, head to the hospital immediately. You will undergo a neurological exam and be watched overnight. If you were unconscious only for a brief time when the injury occurred, you may be able to return to play after you are symptom-free for seven consecutive days. If you were unconscious for a prolonged period of time, you may return to play after you are symptom-free for two consecutive weeks.

➤ If it is your second concussion and it is a grade one concussion, stop playing or practicing immediately. You may return to play after you are symptom-free for seven consecutive days.

➤ If it is your second concussion and it is a grade two concussion, stop playing or practicing immediately. You may return to play after you are symptom-free for two consecutive weeks.

➤ If it is your second concussion and it is a grade three concussion, stop playing or practicing immediately. You may return to play after you are symptom-free for at least a month.

Unfortunately, some coaches will try to coach their athletes on how to trick their physicians into giving them the green light to return to play too soon. To do this, coaches may urge athletes to report that symptoms such as headache or dizziness are gone when in fact they still remain. Do not fall into this trap. Because they involve the brain, head injuries should never be taken lightly. To protect yourself, never lie to a physician about how you feel after a head injury. Allow the appropriate amount of time for rest and recovery.

When it comes to determining where you are in concussion recovery and, therefore, when you should return to play, neuropsychological testing can be very helpful. Neuropsychological tests are used by physicians to measure brain function. Your physician may use any one of a number of available neuropsychological tests to help determine the extent of your head injury and where you are in the healing process.

Post-concussion side effects. Many people who have suffered a concussion experience what is called *post-concussion syndrome*. This condition is far more common in athletes who return to activity too soon. Most common symptoms include fatigue, weakness, headaches, balance/equilibrium disturbances or difficulty in concentrating that may persist for weeks to months after the initial injury. Anyone who continues to experience symptoms of concussion for more than a week or two after the injury should be considered a candidate for further evaluation, including imaging or neuropsychological testing. Symptoms often clear up for a little while but then reappear when the person becomes active again.

If you've suffered a concussion and your symptoms return on the field or court, stop all activity immediately and rest. Post-concussion syndrome is an indication that you need a longer period of rest to recover from the injury. You should never "play through" these symptoms; you should not return to your sport until the symptoms are gone completely.

In addition, people who have suffered a concussion often develop what are known as post-traumatic headaches that typically set in within seven days of the injury and may last for months. These headaches may feel similar to migraines or tension headaches.

There is also the risk for post-traumatic epilepsy (seizures) after a concussion. People who have suffered a concussion have twice the risk of epilepsy in the five years following their injuries. Half of post-traumatic epileptic seizures will happen in the first year, and 80 percent will take place within two years of the head injury.

SKULL FRACTURE

If you experience a very hard hit to the head after a blow or fall, you can fracture the bones of your skull. Although rare, skull fractures can occur during high school sports, and when they do, they present an emergency situation. The depressed skull bone can put pressure on the brain and cause bleeding, coma, or even death.

Symptoms of a skull fracture include clear fluid leaking from the nose or ear.

If you suspect a skull fracture, call an ambulance right away—a trip to the emergency room is in order. At the hospital, the physician will order an imaging study, most likely a CT scan, to diagnose a skull fracture. Depending on the severity of the fracture, treatment will include rest or surgery.

BROKEN NOSE

Any hit to the nose during sports play can lead to a fracture of the nasal bones or the cartilage of the septum (the area that divides your nostrils). Symptoms of a broken nose include a nose that appears crooked or flattened, bleeding from the nose, and difficulty breathing.

To treat a broken nose, first apply ice to decrease swelling and to help prevent bruising. Then head to the hospital. There physicians will examine and X-ray your nose, and if it has been displaced, they will reset it. (If a broken nose is not reset, it can cause breathing problems in the future.) After your nose is reset, you will wear a splint on it until it heals, usually for four to six weeks.

BLOWOUT FRACTURE

A blow to the eye or cheek can result in what's called a *blowout fracture*, a fracture to the bones surrounding the eyeball. If you've suffered a blowout fracture, the injured eye will immediately swell shut. As with other types of fractures, immediate medical care is in order. Treatment may include surgery; in severe cases, a blowout fracture can trap one of the eye muscles, causing double vision unless it is corrected with surgery.

SCRATCHED CORNEA

A scratched cornea frequently occurs after you've been poked in the eye. A common basketball injury, a scratched cornea can be extremely painful, but it is usually minor. However, if the injury is not properly cared for, it can lead to a loss of vision. If you've been poked in the eye and suspect you've suffered a scratched cornea, cover your eye with a patch and see your doctor as soon as possible. He or she will confirm the injury with special staining drops, then treat the scratch using antibiotic eye drops or ointments, medicine to dilate the pupil and promote healing, and/or a temporary eye patch to protect the injured eye.

CAULIFLOWER EAR

A common injury in wrestlers, *cauliflower* ear occurs when the ear is frequently bent over or punched during wrestling holds. As a result, blood pools under the skin, and the ear swells, taking on the appearance of a cauliflower.

If this occurs, you should first ice it and use compression to limit the bleeding, then see a physician to have the excess blood drained as soon as possible. This procedure is followed by firm compression that must be maintained to prevent blood from reaccumulating.

If proper drainage of the blood is not done promptly, or if effective compression is not maintained after the drainage, then a permanent deformity may develop in the ear cartilage. This creates a permanent cauliflower ear that can be fixed only with plastic surgery.

Therefore, prevention is the best strategy when it comes to cauliflower ear. To prevent the condition, wear appropriate headgear during wrestling competitions.

JAW FRACTURE

A broken jaw can result from a blow to the face. If your jaw is indeed broken, your teeth will not meet properly when you clench your jaw, or you may not be able to clench your jaw because of the pain. Treatment of a broken jaw involves having it wired shut by a dental surgeon to allow it to heal. This process usually takes six weeks or so.

You may be able to return to your sport while your jaw is wired shut, but the liquid diet required by the procedure may leave you weaker than usual.

To help prevent a broken jaw, wear a mouthpiece—it will protect your teeth and jaw and disperse the shock from any blow to the area. Mouthpieces are particularly important in sports where elbows fly, such as football, hockey, basketball, and racquetball. Although any mouthpiece is better than none, keep in mind that the rubber or plastic mouthpieces that you buy in the drugstore and heat to fit your teeth at home are not as effective as the customized ones.

TOOTH LOSS

It is not uncommon for an athlete to lose a tooth, particularly during contact sports. Another player's elbow, a stick, or other object can easily cause you to lose or break your tooth. If this happens, you should do your best to find the missing tooth and get to a dentist immediately for reattachment. While in transit, the best place to store the tooth is in your mouth or in milk. You should not place the tooth in plain water. The tooth can often be effectively reattached if these steps are followed and it is treated immediately.

NECK INJURIES

Neck injuries are among the most dangerous of all injuries suffered by teenage athletes. While some injuries may be minor, severe neck injuries can end sports careers, or cause paralysis or even death.

Common neck injuries include strains, fractures, contusions, sprains, and burners (stingers).

By virtue of its position, the neck is much more prone to injury than the rest of the spine. Plus, the muscles that support the neck are much weaker than those that surround the spine lower in the back.

Most neck injuries occur on an acute basis, after a sudden impact to the head or neck as a result of a fall or blow. But neck injuries can also take place slowly, over time. Too much strain on your neck can cause increasing pain on one or both sides of your neck. Sometimes you may feel pain only when you move your head a certain way.

If you hurt yourself on the playing field or court and you suspect a neck injury, the most important thing you can do is lie still and hold your head straight while someone calls for medical help. If you are lying on the ground, do not try to move, and do not let anyone else move you. Stay where you are until an ambulance or EMT crew arrives. A mishandled neck fracture could lead to paralysis, or in severe cases, even death.

NECK FRACTURE (BROKEN NECK)

The most serious of neck injuries, a broken neck describes damaged vertebrae in the neck, usually from a head-on blow or a blow to the head when the neck is bent down, as when a football tackler ducks his head as he makes contact (spear tackling). Each year, a few high school football players suffer broken necks that leave them paralyzed from the neck down. In the high school sports setting, broken necks are also often caused by diving, typically when a diver misjudges the depth of the pool and hits the bottom with his or her head. A broken neck is an emergency requiring immediate medical attention.

Treatment for a broken neck will depend upon the severity of the injury. It may include wearing a cervical collar (soft neck brace) for six to eight weeks, traction, surgery, or a rigid frame to keep the neck from moving. Once the neck has healed, physical therapy helps increase strength and flexibility in the neck.

SPRAINED NECK

When an action causes the head to snap backward, the ligaments that hold the vertebrae in the neck together can be sprained (stretched) or torn. If the injury is severe, a vertebra may slide out of place and compress the spinal cord—the same injury that occurs with a neck fracture. A mild neck sprain will lead to pain and stiffness in the neck area. If your symptoms are any more severe, you should see a doctor.

Treatment for a sprained neck may include immobilization with a cervical collar, pain medications, nonsteroidal anti-inflammatory drugs, and/or muscle relaxants.

STRAINED NECK

Much like muscles in other parts of the body, the muscles that support the neck can get strained with certain activities. This may occur suddenly (for example, during a headlock in wrestling), or may occur over time (such as while cycling with your head held forward for a long time). Muscles in the neck are more vulnerable to strains if they are not strong enough. Since muscles serve to stabilize the neck and protect the ligaments and bones, muscle strains will also typically occur whenever there is a sprain or fracture.

PINCHED NERVE

If your sport makes you prone to violent neck motions, you are at risk for a pinched nerve. A pinched nerve occurs when a cervical *disc* ruptures, and the jellylike material from inside the disc presses on a nerve. Although the problem is in your neck, a pinched nerve frequently causes pain that shoots down into your arm. The pain may come on slowly or suddenly.

One form of a pinched nerve is a stinger (also called a burner). There are two types of stingers—compression stingers and distraction stingers. Compression stingers are the result of compression of a nerve in the neck, so they fall into the category of a pinched nerve.

Treatment of a pinched nerve usually involves cervical traction for two to six weeks. Physical therapy may also help to reduce the resulting muscle spasms. If symptoms don't go away, or the pain continues in your arm or your hand, surgery may be required.

BURNER

A burner (also called a stinger) is a sudden burning pain and a feeling of weakness that shoots down one arm. Burners are common; one survey found that 65 percent of college football players reported experiencing at least one burner in their careers. In some cases, burners can become a recurrent injury. A study of college football players found that 87 percent of those who had suffered a burner experienced at least one more.

These injuries, which occur most frequently in football, wrestling, gymnastics, and hockey, are caused by a pinched nerve in the neck, and they usually come and go within a few minutes. Burners usually go away on their own, and they rarely require medical attention. Nevertheless, if you experience a burner on the playing field, you should have it checked by your school's trainer to rule out something more serious. If the trainer gives you the green light, once you regain the full strength, function, and motion in your arm, you can immediately return to play. If you still experience any symptoms a week later, see your doctor. If the burn persists, you may have a more severe injury—a stretched nerve—that will require rehabilitation and extended time on the bench. If a burner lingers more than three weeks, your physician will likely order an electrodiagnostic study to take a closer look at the injury.

To prevent burners, you should work on flexibility and strength in your neck because stiffness and weakness will predispose you to this injury. You should also have your posture and playing style evaluated by a physical therapist to make sure your technique isn't putting you at risk for future injury. In addition, make sure you wear the appropriate protective equipment and that it fits properly. For instance, football shoulder pads that ride high can significantly reduce your risk of burners.

If you experience recurrent burners, you may want to consider using extra protective equipment, such as a neck roll or Cowboy Collar. Also, be sure to mention your recurrent burners during your annual pre-participation exam; the examining physician may be able to offer some techniques to help you improve range of motion and strength or refer you to a physical therapist.

WHIPLASH

Whiplash is caused by a trauma that leads to an abrupt flexion/extension motion of the neck. Whiplash can affect multiple areas of the neck, including the discs, nerves, ligaments, soft tissues, and other structures. Therefore, much of what we just discussed regarding strains and sprains will occur during whiplash injuries.

When you seek medical attention for whiplash, diagnostic studies may not reveal a problem, but the pain that goes along with the injury can be persistent and disabling.

Treatment for whiplash may include pain medications, nonsteroidal anti-inflammatory drugs, muscle relaxants, physical therapy, and/or the use of a cervical collar.

Although some physicians discourage their use, a soft cervical collar may help during periods of increased pain, particularly if you're having problems sleeping. To avoid muscle weakness, these collars should only be used for two to three hours at a time, however, and not for more than one to two weeks.

PREVENTING HEAD AND NECK INJURIES

Although some prevention strategies are injury-specific, in general you can help to prevent head and neck injuries by doing the following:

▸ Wear appropriate headgear that fits properly and is in good condition for contact sports. Whenever appropriate, WEAR A HELMET. This is the single most important action you can take to prevent a head or neck injury.
▸ Follow rules against dangerous practices, such as butt blocking and face and head tackling (or spear tackling) in football.
▸ Use protective headgear during noncontact sports that carry the risk of head injury, such as skateboarding, snowboarding, rollerblading, and bicycling.
▸ Work on strength and flexibility in your neck to increase strength and range of motion.

Here are some exercises for you to try:

Neck strengthening exercises:
▸ Press your palms against your forehead and push your forehead into your palms and your palms into your forehead at the same time, resisting motion. Hold the position for five seconds and repeat it five times.
▸ Place your hand against the side of your head and try to bring your ear to your shoulder, resisting the motion. Hold the position for five seconds, then relax slowly. Repeat on the other side.
▸ Cup both of your hands against the back of your head and try to push your head back, resisting the motion. Hold for five seconds, then relax slowly.
▸ Put your right hand against your right temple. Try to turn your chin toward your right shoulder, resisting the motion with your hand. Hold for five seconds, then relax slowly. Repeat three times, then switch sides.

Neck stretching exercises:
▸ Bring your chin to your chest (called cervical flexion), then look up to the ceiling (called cervical extension). Start by tucking your chin, bringing your head forward, and attempting to

touch your chin to your chest. Then gently bend your head backward as far as you can. Repeat five times.

➤ Lateral flexion: Bring your right ear to your right shoulder as far as you can without rotating or turning your head. Then switch and do the exercise on the left side. Repeat five times.

➤ Rotation of the cervical spine: Turn your head to the right as far as you can, trying to bring your chin over your shoulders. Do not bring up your shoulders. Hold for three to five seconds. Do this on the left side and repeat both sides five times.

➤ Stand with your feet shoulder-width apart and place your hands behind your head. Bend from side to side with your upper back area only, not with your waist or hips. As you are bending, try to reach your upper elbow to the ceiling. Hold each stretch for three to five seconds and repeat on the other side.

WHAT YOU NEED TO KNOW

➤ Since your head houses your brain and, therefore, all your body's central control centers, any injury to the head that appears to be more severe than a mild bump or scrape should be seen by a doctor.

➤ Even if you look and appear fine after a concussion, you should be monitored for 24 hours for symptoms such as headache, nausea, and further loss of consciousness.

➤ If you are unconscious for an extended period of time (more than a few seconds) or you do not recover from the blow to your head immediately, seek medical attention.

➤ Symptoms of a skull fracture include clear fluid leaking from the nose or ear. If you suspect a skull fracture, call an ambulance right away.

➤ If you've been poked in the eye and suspect you've suffered a scratched cornea, cover your eye with a patch and see your doctor as soon as possible.

➤ If you hurt yourself on the playing field or court and you suspect a neck injury, the most important thing you can do is lie still and hold your head straight while someone calls for medical help.

➤ A mild neck sprain will lead to pain and stiffness in the neck area. If your symptoms are any more severe than this, you should see a doctor.

➤ You can help to prevent head and neck injuries by wearing appropriate protective headgear that fits properly and by following rules against dangerous practices.

4 ▌▌▌

Shoulder Injuries

As she fell from the balance beam and hit the mat, Tori, 14, heard her shoulder pop. When she stood up, she felt a sharp pain as the head of her shoulder slipped back into its socket. For the weeks following, Tori noticed a similar sharp pain whenever she raised her arms over her head during her floor routine. She also found herself approaching her handsprings with trepidation, fearing that she'd bring on the same uncomfortable sensation in her shoulder.

Tired of her shoulder instability getting in the way of her performance in gymnastics meets, Tori saw her doctor, who diagnosed a shoulder *dislocation* and prescribed exercises to help stretch and strengthen her shoulder. After six weeks of performing the exercises as diligently as she approached her gymnastics training, Tori regained the strength and stability in her shoulder. Today, she's back to competing at the same level she was before her fall.

Tori is certainly not the first teenage athlete to suffer a shoulder dislocation. Each year, thousands of high school athletes suffer shoulder injuries, dislocations included.

This chapter will cover some of the most common shoulder injuries in teens, including injuries to the acromioclavicular joint, subluxations, dislocations, rotator cuff and other muscle/tendon injuries, broken collarbones, general shoulder instability, as well as offer advice on how teenage athletes can best prevent and treat them.

44

INTRODUCTION TO SHOULDER INJURIES

By virtue of its shape and construction, the shoulder is vulnerable to a number of sports-related injuries. Anatomically, the shoulder consists of a shallow ball and socket joint, in which the ball has little contact with the small socket, so it can easily slide out. Ligaments and cartilage make up the rest of the socket, and the ligaments prevent the shoulder from moving too far in one direction. The two main bones of the shoulder are the *humerus* (the bone between the shoulder and the elbow) and the *scapula* (shoulder blade). Ligaments hold together the bones of the shoulder, and the tendons connect the bones to surrounding muscles. The biceps tendon also passes through the shoulder joint and helps to stabilize the joint.

Above the ball and socket joint of the shoulder is a separate joint called the *acromioclavicular* (AC) *joint,* which joins the scapula to the collarbone (clavicle), and is subject to injury, especially through direct trauma. Below the shoulder socket is the brachial plexus, the home of all the nerves of the arm.

The shoulder bones are held together by a group of four muscles called the rotator cuff muscles, which include the supraspinatus, infraspinatus, teres minor, and subscapularis. When these muscles become weak, the shoulder can easily slide partially out of the socket—called a subluxation—or all the way out of the socket, which is a full shoulder dislocation. The rotator cuff is a popular site of injury in high school athletes, particularly in sports that involve throwing and other overhead arm motions.

Considering the shoulder's somewhat vulnerable construction, it's no wonder so many high school athletes suffer from shoulder injuries. Most sports can cause shoulder injuries—some acute, some chronic. Chances are, you know at least one classmate who has suffered from some sort of injury to his or her shoulder.

Most sports can, in some way, lead to shoulder injuries, though some sports carry an increased risk of injury. These sports include baseball, softball, basketball, football, rugby, golf, gymnastics, cheerleading, hockey, lacrosse, track and field, swimming, tennis, volleyball, and wrestling.

Here is an overview of some of the most common shoulder injuries in teenage athletes:

ACROMIOCLAVICULAR JOINT INJURIES

The acromioclavicular (AC) joint, which joins the collarbone and the shoulder blade, is a frequent shoulder injury site in high school athletes. Although the AC joint is strong, its location makes it vulnerable to injury, especially from direct trauma, such as a fall on or a blow to the shoulder. A fall on an outstretched arm or elbow can also damage the AC joint. AC joint injuries can also occur when the cartilage between the collarbone and the shoulder blade wears away, causing bone to rub on bone.

Weight lifters—particularly those who perform bench presses or overhead lifting using heavy weights—frequently suffer AC joint strains. In the case of strength training, the AC joint isn't injured by way of a fall or blow—rather, the weight lifter lifts improperly or adds too much weight too fast. Weight lifters who train on their own are more likely to strain an AC joint than athletes who are trained on proper lifting techniques. The two most common causes of AC joint tears in weight lifters are trying to lift too much weight too fast, and not placing the hands correctly on the bar.

As with all sprains, AC joint sprains can be mild (first-degree), moderate (second-degree), or severe (third-degree). Symptoms of all three degrees usually include swelling, pain, and possible deformity of the joint.

A first-degree or type I sprain causes a mild stretching and possibly minor tearing of the ligaments. Symptoms include pain and swelling around the joint immediately following the injury, but no deformity.

A second-degree or type II sprain stretches and partially tears the ligaments so that the shoulder becomes springy and unstable. Symptoms include pain and significant swelling.

With a third-degree or type III sprain, the ligaments may be so damaged that there is an obvious deformity; there will be a visible bump on the collarbone in addition to the swelling. Symptoms include severe pain and swelling and obvious displacement of the collarbone.

There are also type IV, V, and VI AC joint injuries—some are so severe that the bone protrudes through the skin—but these types of injuries are unusual. If any type of shoulder injury leads to bone protrusion, head to the emergency room immediately.

These injuries should all, at some point, be evaluated by a doctor, sooner than later if you suspect a more severe injury such as a type III AC joint sprain. He or she will examine your shoulder for signs of a sprain and possibly X-ray the area to confirm the diagnosis.

For mild and moderate AC joint sprains, treatment usually involves a few days of icing the area on and off, followed by a few weeks of rest, over-the-counter anti-inflammatory medications, and in some cases, a cortisone shot. Depending on the severity of the injury, rest may involve immobilizing the shoulder in a sling for a few weeks.

Rehabilitative exercises will also likely be prescribed. It may take a few weeks for the sprain to heal, during which time you may not be able to raise your arm laterally beyond 90 degrees.

With permission from your doctor, you can return to play following a mild AC joint sprain as soon as you can practice your sport without pain. For most athletes, this is between three days and two weeks following the sprain, depending on the severity. Athletes who practice overhead throwing as part of their sports—baseball players, pitchers,

What Are Burners and What Causes Them?

A burner (also called a stinger) is a sudden burning pain and a feeling of weakness that shoots down one arm. These injuries, which occur most frequently in football, wrestling, gymnastics, and hockey, are caused by stretching of the nerves in the arm.

Burners usually go away on their own without treatment, and they rarely require further medical attention. Nevertheless, if you experience a burner on the playing field, you should have it checked by your school's trainer to rule out something more serious. If the trainer gives you the green light, once you regain the full strength, function, and motion in your arm, you can immediately return to play. If you still experience symptoms a week later, see your doctor to rule out something more serious. If the burn persists, you may have a more severe injury that will require rehabilitation and extended time on the bench. If a burner lingers more than three weeks, your physician will likely order an electrodiagnostic study of the nerves (EMG) to take a closer look at the injury.

To prevent burners, you should work on flexibility and strength in your neck, chest, and shoulders because stiffness and weakness will predispose you to this injury. You should also have your posture and playing style evaluated by a physical therapist to make sure your technique isn't putting you at risk for future injury. In addition, make sure you wear the appropriate protective equipment and that it fits properly. For instance, football shoulder pads that ride high can significantly reduce your risk of burners.

volleyball players, and tennis players—may need to rest for up to six weeks, however.

Treatment for second-degree AC joint sprains usually includes rest, ice, over-the-counter or prescription anti-inflammatory medications, and three to seven days of immobilization in a sling. As with first-degree sprains, athletes can usually return to play as soon as they can comfortably practice and play their sports, which typically takes two to four weeks. Complete healing of the ligaments may take longer.

When it comes to third-degree AC joint sprains, initial treatment also includes rest, ice, immobilization, and over-the-counter or prescription anti-inflammatory medications. You can begin strengthening exercises as soon as they are comfortable. In severe cases, surgery may be necessary, although surgery to treat AC joint injuries is rare. If surgery is prescribed, you will typically need to rest the joint for six weeks following the procedure, then start strengthening exercises to rehabilitate the joint.

As with first- and second-degree AC sprains, athletes with third-degree AC sprains who do not require surgery can return to play when they have regained sufficient strength and range of motion, usually within six to 12 weeks.

ROTATOR CUFF/BICEPS STRAINS

Rotator cuff injuries are extremely common in teenage athletes; in fact, they are the most common shoulder injuries for which patients seek treatment.

In teenage athletes, rotator cuff injuries typically result from overhead arm activity. The shoulder joint is not designed to frequently allow the arm to rise above a line parallel to the ground. The rotator cuff muscles help stabilize the shoulder joint—in other words, hold the ball down in its socket—during throwing and other motions. Therefore, sports that require athletes to bring their arms up over their heads, such as tennis, volleyball, golf, gymnastics, swimming, and baseball, result in excessive repetitive movement within the shoulder joint, stressing the rotator cuff muscles. Over time, these muscles become damaged, often along with the ligaments that become stretched out, allowing the head of the shoulder joint to become loose within the socket. When the shoulder head becomes loose, it slides forward whenever you move your arm backward over your shoulder (picture a baseball player winding up for a pitch), or when you raise your arm higher than a line parallel to the ground, and the tendons of the short head or long head of the biceps get caught between the ball and socket.

When these tendons get pinched, they become inflamed and painful. The area where an athlete feels this pain often depends on his or her sport. For instance, tennis players may feel the pain in different places than swimmers or baseball players.

To diagnose a rotator cuff strain and eliminate other potential causes of shoulder pain, doctors will usually perform a physical examination and conduct one or more tests, including range-of-motion tests, strength tests, and others. They may also order an X-ray, ultrasound, or MRI to visually assess what's going on.

Treatment for a rotator cuff or biceps strain generally includes rest, ice, and over-the-counter or prescription anti-inflammatory medications, followed by an intensive specific strengthening program (often with physical therapist), once ready. Some doctors will treat rotator cuff strains with cortisone injections, or order ultrasound, or electrical stimulation to be done by the physical therapist. Although these remedies will work in the short term, the most important part of the treatment for a rotator cuff strain is to practice exercises that strengthen the muscles so the head of the shoulder stays in place in its socket. In fact, an estimated three out of four rotator cuff strains can be cured with exercise alone. When the head stays in place, it takes the strain off the surrounding ligaments and tendons. Since all muscles in the shoulder joint work together, it is also very important to strengthen the scapular stabilizer muscles (serratus anterior, lower trapezius, rhomboids, etc.).

Depending on the extent of your rotator cuff or biceps injury, your doctor may refer you to a physical therapist, or he or she may simply instruct you to do shoulder-strengthening exercises on your own. If you don't have complete relief after six to nine months, surgery may be in order. Surgery is very rarely required to repair rotator cuff injuries, however, especially in young athletes.

You will get the green light to return to play after a rotator cuff strain when you can exhibit full range of motion and have regained strength and stability in your shoulder.

ROTATOR CUFF TEAR

In some cases, shoulder pain may be due to a torn rotator cuff rather than just a strained one. Symptoms of a rotator cuff tear include pain and weakness. The pain may get worse when you perform overhead activities, and at night if you lie on your shoulder. In some athletes, rotator cuff tears produce no pain, however, in which case weakness is the only symptom.

If you suspect that you have torn your rotator cuff, see your doctor. He or she will perform specific physical exams and may order an MRI or ultrasound to confirm that you indeed have a rotator cuff tear.

Some tears can be treated similarly to strains, with proper strengthening exercises. In the case of a more severe tear that does not respond to physical therapy, however, treatment may involve surgery. Luckily, there are less invasive surgeries available today that can completely repair a rotator cuff tear, which may have once ended an athletic career.

You should think hard before agreeing to surgery for a rotator cuff injury, however, because all of the surgical options available involve a fairly difficult recovery. Because you must rest your shoulder for four to six weeks after surgery, your shoulder can lose its ability to move and become frozen, requiring a long, painful rehabilitation program. Never hesitate to get a second opinion before undergoing surgery.

Return to play after a rotator cuff injury depends on the severity of the injury. If the rotator cuff isn't completely torn and surgery isn't involved, most athletes can return to play within six weeks. If there is a complete tear and surgery is required, return to play will take several months.

SHOULDER MUSCLE PULL

When the rotator cuff muscles become strained or torn, surrounding muscles can be injured as well. These muscles include the deltoids, trapezius, biceps, latissimus dorsi, and others.

Shoulder muscle pulls can also occur independently of rotator cuff injuries. Because the shoulder is used so often in athletics, and because it contains ligaments, tendons, and muscles, it is vulnerable to pulls.

With a shoulder muscle pull, the muscles overstretch, which causes the muscle fibers to tear. High school wrestlers and baseball and softball pitchers tend to be most vulnerable to shoulder muscle pulls.

If you pull a shoulder muscle, see your doctor; a shoulder pull is not an injury that you should try to treat on your own. Symptoms of a shoulder muscle pull mimic those of much more serious shoulder injuries, so you should get a professional diagnosis. Also, your physician will be able to determine the exact muscles you've pulled and, therefore, prescribe exercises that will target those specific muscles. The initial treatment will involve ice for a few days and rest for up to a week, followed by muscle-specific exercises to help stretch and strengthen your shoulder.

To prevent a shoulder muscle pull, be sure to warm up properly and stretch your shoulders before you work out, practice, or compete.

SHOULDER DISLOCATION

Shoulder dislocations are extremely common in high school athletes, accounting for about half of all major joint dislocations. Up to 97 percent of shoulder dislocations are anterior (front) as opposed to posterior (back) dislocations. Anterior dislocations are most often caused by a blow to an extended arm, such as when a basketball player is hit in the arm when he or she is trying to block a shot. Posterior dislocations, which may be caused by a blow to the front of the shoulder, are much less common.

If you suspect a shoulder dislocation, see a doctor. He or she will examine your shoulder and order an X-ray. Depending on the severity of the injury, you may be diagnosed with a partial dislocation (called a subluxation), or a complete shoulder dislocation.

SUBLUXATION

In cases in which an athlete suffers a sudden force against his or her shoulder, the head of the shoulder can slip temporarily out of the socket—called a partial dislocation or a *subluxation*. Sports that frequently lead to subluxations include football, swimming, gymnastics, tennis, volleyball, and wrestling.

With a subluxation, the shoulder feels as though it popped out of the socket and then popped back in. In the case of a partial dislocation, however, the shoulder doesn't actually pop out of the socket—if it did, it wouldn't slip back in on its own.

The problem with shoulder subluxations is that they can become chronic, repeatedly stretching your shoulder muscles and making you vulnerable to more subluxations. The stretched muscles also allow your shoulder to slide around, which can lead to shoulder impingement and tendonitis. Eventually, the shoulder muscles can become so stretched that you are at risk for a total shoulder dislocation.

To treat a subluxation, your doctor will first prescribe rest and an exercise program to strengthen your rotator cuff muscles. Unfortunately, the muscles in the shoulder are slow to heal, and depending on the extent of the subluxation, you could be out of your sport for six to 12 weeks, or up to six months or more.

The Importance of Scapular Stabilization

One factor commonly overlooked by physicians, trainers, and physical therapists when it comes to preventing shoulder injuries is the importance of scapular stabilization. The scapula—shoulder blade—is held in place by numerous muscles, including the serratus anterior, rhomboids, lower trapezius, and pectoralis minor. When the scapula fails to perform its role in helping to stabilize the shoulder, an athlete becomes vulnerable to shoulder injuries. Therefore, scapular stabilization and strengthening are crucial when rehabilitating the shoulder. In addition, the scapula is an important part of preventing shoulder injuries and improving sports performance, particularly when it comes to throwing and pitching. Here are a few exercises that can help to keep your shoulder blades strong:

Shoulder roll (can do this exercise with or without light dumbbells)
Stand with your feet shoulder-width apart and your arms at your sides. Move your shoulders forward, shrug your shoulders up, then move your shoulders backward. Then squeeze your shoulder blades together and pull your shoulders downward. Repeat five times. Repeat the shoulder roll five times in the opposite direction—your shoulders backward, shoulders up, shoulders forward, in one continuous circular motion. As your strength increases, do another set. Rest for 30 seconds between sets.

Wall push-ups
Stand about 18 inches away from a wall. Place your hands on the wall at shoulder level. Slowly lower yourself toward the wall and return to the starting position. To make this exercise more difficult, use progressively lower surfaces—counter, tabletop, etc.

Press
Lie on your back. Raise one arm straight in the air, lifting it higher until your shoulder blade is off the ground. Repeat 10 times, then switch sides. As your strength increases, add a light dumbbell.

FULL SHOULDER DISLOCATION

A shoulder becomes fully dislocated if the blow to the area is so forceful that it causes the shoulder head to slip all the way out of its socket or your arm is stretched in such a way that the ball is forced out of the socket. In some cases, a dislocation merely stretches the rotator cuff muscles. Younger athletes who suffer shoulder dislocations often get by with only stretched rotator cuff muscles. In older athletes, however, a dislocation is more likely to lead to a full rotator cuff or cartilage tear. Shoulder dislocations occur more frequently in athletes with inherent laxity (looseness) of their ligaments or prior dislocations. Sports that most frequently lead to shoulder dislocations include football, wrestling, gymnastics, cheerleading, some weight lifting, downhill skiing, and any other sport that may place the shoulder in an unexpected, compromising position.

Symptoms of a dislocated shoulder include severe pain and an arm that appears slightly rotated. Treatment first involves what is called a reduction, where the physician snaps the joint back in place using one of a number of different techniques. If you dislocated your shoulder within the last 24 hours or if it is the result of a recurrent injury, the physician may perform the reduction without a sedative or painkiller. The reduction may hurt temporarily, but it will ultimately relieve the pain. If it is a first-time dislocation, the physician may use a local anesthetic to numb the area before performing the reduction.

Following the reduction, your doctor will most likely prescribe a few weeks of immobilization in a sling that you wear at all times except to bathe, and perhaps more important, exercises to strengthen the surrounding muscles. He or she may also refer you to an orthopedic surgeon for a follow-up evaluation. For athletes who suffer repeated shoulder dislocations, or in cases where a physician cannot reduce a dislocation, surgery may be necessary.

In most cases, athletes can return to play following a shoulder dislocation after about 12 to 16 weeks.

Unfortunately, 50 to 90 percent of teenage athletes who suffer one shoulder dislocation will experience another one. You can help to prevent a recurrent dislocation by immobilizing your shoulder for a longer period of time following your first dislocation, engaging in shoulder-strengthening exercises as part of a physical therapy program, and in severe cases by having surgery. Surgery may also be necessary.

Many athletes who suffer repeated shoulder dislocations try to reduce them on their own. This is not generally recommended and certainly should not be done without the OK and instructions from a doctor, as it may cause damage to surrounding structures if done improperly. A common technique used is clasping your hands around your flexed knee in a seated position, then leaning back slowly and extending your hip (pausing if the pain becomes unbearable) until the joint pops back into place.

Keep in mind that repeated shoulder dislocations—partial or total—put you at risk for other shoulder injuries. Here are two specific injuries that may result from repeated shoulder dislocations:

BANKART LESION

A *Bankart lesion* is an injury to part of the shoulder joint at an area called the *labrum*. The labrum is a cuff of cartilage that forms a cup that the humerus (arm bone) moves within. When a person sustains a shoulder dislocation, the shoulder can tear the labrum as it pops out of the joint. In the case of a Bankart lesion, a part of the labrum called the inferior glenohumeral ligament gets torn.

Teenagers are particularly vulnerable to Bankart lesions. In fact, most athletes under the age of 30 will sustain a Bankart lesion when they dislocate a shoulder.

Symptoms of a Bankart lesion include aching in the shoulder, a "catching" sensation when moving the shoulder, a sense of instability, and repeated dislocations. If you have a Bankart lesion, you may not fully trust your shoulder, and you may constantly fear that you will dislocate it again.

To diagnose a Bankart lesion, your doctor will perform a physical exam and order an X-ray and/or an MRI. (Bankart lesions often do not show up on MRIs, however.)

If a Bankart lesion is confirmed, treatment will involve resting your arm and shoulder, possibly with the aid of a sling. In most cases, rest is followed with physical therapy to regain motion in the shoulder and to strengthen the area. In severe cases, surgery may be necessary.

HILL-SACHS LESION

A *Hill-Sachs lesion* is a divot of the humerus (arm bone) that gets injured during a shoulder dislocation. Specifically, when the shoulder dislocates, the cartilage of the humerus gets trapped against the shoulder joint.

To diagnose a Hill-Sachs lesion, your physician will order an X-ray. In most cases, treatment will involve rest and anti-inflammatory medications only, but if the injury is severe or associated with significant shoulder instability, surgery may be required.

SHOULDER INSTABILITY

Shoulder instability, or "loose shoulder" in teenage athletes often results from repeated subluxations or other shoulder injuries. Athletes with shoulder instability have a shoulder that repeatedly slips, pops out of the socket, and/or feels weak. Shoulder instability is most common in teenage athletes who participate in swimming or throwing sports.

Symptoms of shoulder instability may include pain, numbness, tingling, or weakness in one or both shoulders that worsens with some activities. Athletes with shoulder instability will be reluctant to move their affected arms in certain directions, and they may experience popping and/or the sensation that the shoulders will dislocate, or pain in the rotator cuff or biceps tendons. Some people will also have instability in other joints.

To diagnose shoulder instability, a physician will typically perform a physical examination, and in some cases, an X-ray or MRI.

If shoulder instability is confirmed, initial treatment will include rest, specifically restriction of overhead reaching, pushing, lifting, and pulling. Ice and anti-inflammatory medications may also be prescribed.

Your physician will also likely instruct you to perform daily shoulder-strengthening exercises. If you don't improve in two to four weeks, your physician may also prescribe cortisone injections. There are even some alternative procedures such as prolotherapy, in which a physician specially trained in the procedure will inject an irritating substance (often sugar water) into the loose ligament with the intent of causing inflammation, followed by strengthening of the ligament. This often involves a series of injections spaced a few weeks apart. If pain persists, surgery may be considered.

SLAP TEARS

A SLAP tear (SLAP stands for Superior Labrum from Anterior to Posterior) is an injury to part of the shoulder joint called the labrum. The labrum is a cuff of cartilage that forms a cup that the humerus (arm bone) moves within. A SLAP tear occurs at the point that the tendon of the biceps muscle joins with the labrum. SLAP tears frequently result from a dislocation or repetitive overhead actions such as throwing and heavy lifting.

Symptoms of a SLAP tear include pain and a "catching" sensation when you move your shoulder. The pain often feels as if it is deep within the shoulder joint.

If you suspect a SLAP tear, see your doctor. He or she will ask you questions about how the injury occurred, perform a physical examination, and use specific tests to help pinpoint the location of your injury. He or she may also order an MRI to help confirm the diagnosis.

To treat a SLAP tear, you will be advised to rest your shoulder. Your doctor may also prescribe physical therapy, anti-inflammatory medications, and/or cortisone injections. If your injury doesn't respond to these treatments, surgery may be in order. Return to play following a SLAP tear depends on the severity of the injury.

BROKEN COLLARBONE

A broken collarbone (fractured clavicle) is a common injury among high school athletes. The collarbone doesn't fully harden until about age 20, making teenagers more susceptible to a break. In most cases, a broken collarbone results from a fall that transmits force from the elbow to the shoulder to the collarbone, causing it to break.

Symptoms of a broken collarbone include a sharp pain that gets worse when you move your shoulder or apply pressure to the area. If you suspect a broken collarbone, seek immediate medical attention.

Treatment for a broken collarbone includes a brace to pull and hold the bones in place. It usually takes six to eight weeks for a broken collarbone to heal, but in some cases, the brace may be removed as soon as three weeks. Physical therapy may or may not be necessary.

Return to play following a broken collarbone will depend on the extent of the injury and the sport that caused it. Thanks to better-made shoulder pads, football players may be able to return rather quickly, within a few weeks. Gymnasts, on the other hand, may have to wait longer. No matter what, wait until you get the green light from your physician to practice any activity following a broken collarbone.

EXERCISES TO HELP STRETCH AND STRENGTHEN YOUR SHOULDERS

Standing arm curl. Standing with your feet shoulder-width apart, hold a dumbbell (ask your physician to suggest the proper weight for you) in your right hand with your palm facing forward and your hand at your side. Slowly bend your elbow, lifting the weight to your shoulder. Then slowly lower the weight to the starting position and repeat with the left side.

Front lift, with palm up. Standing with your feet shoulder-width apart, hold a dumbbell in your right hand at your side, with your palm facing forward. Lock your elbow so your arm is straight, then lift the weight straight up until your arm is parallel to the floor. Slowly lower the weight to the starting position and repeat with the left side.

Front lift, with palm down. Standing with your feet shoulder-width apart, hold a dumbbell in your right hand at your side, with your palm facing backward. Lock your elbow so your arm is straight, then lift the weight straight up until your arm is parallel to the floor. Slowly lower the weight to the starting position and repeat with the left side.

Lateral lift. Standing with your feet shoulder-width apart, hold a dumbbell in your right hand, with your palm facing your body. Lock your elbow so your arm is straight, then lift the weight to one side until your arm is parallel with the floor. Slowly lower the weight to the starting position and repeat with the left side.

Bent-over chest lift. Stand with your feet shoulder-width apart and bend over at a 90-degree angle. Hold a dumbbell with your right hand. Lock your elbow so that your arm is straight, then lift the weight across your chest. Slowly lower the weight to the starting position and repeat with the left side.

Bent-over lateral lift. Stand with your feet shoulder-width apart and bend over at a 90-degree angle. Hold a dumbbell with your right hand. Lock your elbow so that your arm is straight, then lift the weight up and to the side until your arm is parallel to the floor. Slowly lower the weight to the starting position and repeat with the left side.

Internal rotation. Lie on one side. Hold a dumbbell on the same side. Bend your elbow at a 90-degree angle and keep your elbow close to your body. Slowly lift the dumbbell upward and toward your body. Pause, then return to the starting position. Repeat 10 times, then repeat on the other side.

External rotation. Lie on your left side. With your right arm, hold a dumbbell next to your body with your elbow bent at 90 degrees. Slowly lift your arm upward until the back of your hand faces backward. Return to the starting position. Repeat 10 times, then repeat on the other side.

Lateral raise. Stand or sit in a chair. With your arms at your side and your thumbs pointed upward, slowly raise your arms to the sides, but slightly toward the front at about a 30-degree angle to the front of your body until almost at shoulder level. Repeat 10 times.

Doorway pectorals stretch. Stand in the middle of a doorway with one foot in front of the other. Bend your elbows to a 90-degree angle and place your forearms on each side of the doorway. Shift your weight to your front leg, leaning forward until you feel a stretch in your chest muscles. Hold for 15 seconds, then relax and return to the starting position. Repeat 10 times.

Door hang stretch. Grasp a door hang so that your body is hanging. Relax and feel the stretch in your shoulders and upper back. Hold for at least 10 to 15 seconds and relax. Repeat two to three times.

Abduction. Stand with your feet shoulder-width apart in front of a mirror. Hold a dumbbell in each hand. Your arms should be at your sides with your palms facing inward toward your legs. Rotate your palms outward as you slowly raise your arms out to the sides of your body 90 degrees. (If you feel pain, stop.) At the top of the lift, rotate your hands back down toward the floor and slowly return your arms back down to the starting position. Do two sets of 10, resting for 30 seconds between each exercise.

WHAT YOU NEED TO KNOW

- Each year, thousands of high school athletes suffer shoulder injuries.
- By virtue of its shape and construction, the shoulder is vulnerable to a number of sports-related injuries.
- Rotator cuff injuries are the most common shoulder injuries in high school athletes.
- Surgery for a rotator cuff injury should be considered carefully as it requires a long, painful rehabilitation program. Don't hesitate to seek a second opinion.
- If you have aching in your shoulder, a "catching" sensation when you move your shoulder, a sense of instability, and repeated dislocations, you could have a more severe injury, such as a SLAP tear or Bankart lesion.
- Symptoms of a broken collarbone include a sharp pain that gets worse when you move your shoulder or apply pressure to the area. If you suspect a broken collarbone, seek medical attention immediately.

- Shoulder-strengthening exercises are important for preventing first or subsequent shoulder dislocations.
- You should never try to diagnose a shoulder muscle pull yourself because symptoms can mimic other more serious shoulder injuries. See your doctor if you suspect a shoulder muscle pull.

5 ▐▐▐

Elbow Injuries

Will, 15, is the star pitcher on his high school's junior varsity baseball team. For the past two weeks, Will has thrown more pitches than he ever has in his eight-year baseball career (he played Little League as a child), and his elbow has begun to feel tight and sore. Assuming his elbow discomfort is due to the temporary increase in his pitching, Will has chosen to ignore the pain and to continue to pitch at the increased pace. After all, the playoffs are coming up, and Will doesn't want to disappoint his coach. Plus, with all the practice, Will has been pitching better than ever, and he doesn't want to lose his winning streak.

The pain and stiffness that Will is feeling in his elbow is definitely not something he should push through, however. Most likely, Will is suffering from *pitcher's elbow,* and rest is in order. If Will doesn't give his elbow a break, the injury will only get worse, ruining his chances of pitching in the playoffs.

INTRODUCTION TO ELBOW INJURIES

The elbow is a very important joint, both in athletics and in everyday life. Take a minute to think about what your life would be like without your elbow. Like a straight-armed Barbie doll, you would only be able to move your arms straight up and down, and you wouldn't be able to rotate your hand from palm down to palm up. You couldn't pull a door shut, hold something in the palm of your hand, or feed yourself.

The ever-so-important elbow is located at the junction of three bones—the humerus (upper arm bone), ulna (larger of the two forearm bones), and radius. The elbow also comprises three separate joints—the junction of the two bones of the forearm, and the junction of these two bones with the bone of the upper arm (the humerus). These three joints—called the radiocapitellar, ulnohumeral, and radioulnar joints—allow the elbow to bend, straighten, and rotate. There are also three ligaments in the elbow joint that help stabilize it—the medial collateral ligament, lateral collateral ligament, and annular ligament.

The muscles of the elbow can be split into two major groups—those that help with flexion/extension, and those that help with supination/pronation. (Flexion is the bending of the arm, and extension is the arm held out straight. *Supination* is the ability to turn the palm upward, and *pronation* is the ability to turn the palm downward.) Some of the muscles in the elbow aid in both flexion/extension and supination/pronation.

The muscles that help with flexion and extension include the biceps, triceps, brachialis, and pronator teres. Muscles that aid in supination/pronation include the biceps, brachioradialis, supinator, and pronator teres.

ELBOW INJURIES IN TEEN ATHLETES

During adolescence, areas of the bone in the elbow known as ossification centers are still fusing; by young adulthood, these areas have fused together to form the bony elbow. Girls tend to be a year ahead of boys in the fusion of these ossification centers. But no matter what your gender, because your elbow is still forming in your teenage years, you are more at risk for sports-related elbow injuries than are adults with mature and fully formed elbows.

Elbow injuries can be chronic or acute. Some elbow injuries result from repeated stress on the elbow; sports such as tennis, racquetball, golf, baseball, and weight lifting stress the elbow joint repeatedly, and these sports can lead to overuse elbow injuries. Athletes who have injured their shoulders, back, or knees in the past are also at an increased risk for overuse elbow injuries, since these injuries may change the biomechanics of their throws or other sports-related motions.

Overuse or chronic elbow injuries develop over time and generally do not pose a medical emergency. Common overuse elbow injuries in teenage athletes include tennis elbow, pitcher's elbow, and Little League elbow. In general, elbow injuries that result from overuse can initially be treated at home using over-the-counter aspirin, acetamino-phen, or *nonsteroidal anti-inflammatory medications* (NSAIDS) and RICE (Rest, Ice, Compression, Elevation). Ice can be applied for about 20 minutes at a time, four to eight times a day.

When it comes to chronic elbow injuries, it's important to note that the most effective part of treatment is addressing the biome-chanics that caused the injury in the first place. For example, when you throw, hit a ball, or perform other elbow motions while playing sports, you often use your hips, torso, and shoulders as well, and incorrect form, weakness, or stiffness in any of those areas during sports play can strain your elbow. Therefore, it's a good idea to talk to your school trainer about having your form analyzed, as well as your strength and flexibility. You should also perform exercises to improve in all these areas.

Acute elbow injuries, or injuries that occur suddenly, tend to result from a fall on an outstretched arm during sports or everyday activi-ties. If you experience a sudden elbow injury that leads to severe pain, swelling, or an inability to move your elbow, seek medical attention immediately. In the meantime, splint the injured arm, secure it with an elastic wrap, and apply ice to the area in 10- to 20-minute intervals until help arrives.

But no matter if they are acute or chronic, elbow injuries shouldn't be taken lightly. Left untreated, elbow injuries can limit sports play, lead to other injuries, and perhaps even lead to permanent problems. For example, elbow injuries can damage the nerve at the end of the elbow joint (the nerve that causes "funny bone" pain) and lead to permanent problems with the forearm, wrist, hand, and fingers. Therefore, if you are having elbow pain, you should see your doctor before continuing to practice or play your sport.

Here are some of the most common elbow injuries in teen ath-letes—split into the main categories of chronic and acute injuries—and what you can do to prevent and treat them.

TENNIS ELBOW

The most common elbow injury, tennis elbow (also called *lateral epicondylitis*), is a repetitive-use injury of the tendon that extends the wrist through the muscles of the forearm and attaches to the outer (lateral) elbow. When you repeatedly bend your wrist back-ward to turn your hand faceup, the muscles and tendons become inflamed from overuse. Tennis elbow tends to occur in athletes who have less experience in their sports, making teenagers particularly at risk.

Tennis elbow is so named for a reason—tennis players are most vulnerable to the injury because of the repeated use of the elbow during play. Novice tennis players are more at risk, due to improper mechanics. Tennis players who hit the ball late on a backhand are most at risk for tennis elbow. The backhand forces a player to shift the weight onto his or her back foot and compensate by bending the elbow and wrist, which strains the muscles and tendons of the forearm.

Golfers are also at risk for tennis elbow, but on their nondominant side. For example, a golfer who is right-handed will feel the pain of tennis elbow on the left arm. The injury results when the golfer pulls the club through the swing with the left wrist.

Other sports that put athletes at risk for tennis elbow include baseball and softball, racquetball, football, rugby, bowling, hockey, lacrosse, skating, swimming and other water sports, volleyball, and wrestling. And certain daily activities—when done repeatedly—can lead to tennis elbow, including typing or using a computer mouse.

Symptoms of tennis elbow include pain on the outside of the elbow that gets worse when you put pressure on it or try to lift things with your palm facing down; for example, you may feel the pain when you pick up a cup to take a drink. You will also feel the pain when you rotate your hand as you would to screw in a light bulb or turn a doorknob, or when you squeeze something like a golf club, a tennis racquet, or someone's hand when you shake it. You may also feel it when you try to wash or comb your hair.

Tennis elbow can also strike the inner side of the elbow, in which case you will feel the pain when you turn your wrist so your palm faces down. Tennis players who develop this type of tennis elbow— also called *medial epicondylitis* or "golfer's elbow"—tend to hit a lot of topspin on their forehand shots, forcing them to snap their wrists. Athletes in sports that also involve wrist snapping—such as baseball, softball, and other throwing sports—are also at risk for this type of tennis elbow, which is discussed in more detail later in the chapter.

If you have tennis elbow, the pain during your everyday activities will soon get to the point that you'll do anything for relief. Simply avoiding playing tennis or the sport that caused your injury unfortunately won't be enough to treat it.

If you suspect either type of tennis elbow, see your doctor. He or she will prescribe special exercises to help increase the strength and flexibility of the muscles and tendon in your forearm. Once these muscles are strong enough, they should be able to withstand the stresses of the sport, though you should still have your technique analyzed since it probably contributed to the injury in the first place.

Your doctor can address the form you use while playing your sport and look at the entire kinetic chain from your hips through your trunk through your shoulders to make sure you are using maximum efficiency in your motion. He or she may also prescribe a tennis elbow brace to wear during activities that stress your sore elbow.

In addition to exercises and a brace, your doctor may prescribe cortisone shots to calm the pain and inflammation. This is only a temporary remedy, however, lasting four to six weeks. For more permanent relief, you and your doctor should consider other treatment options.

Additional remedies for tennis elbow include deep friction massage to increase blood flow to the area and promote healing, and *iontophoresis,* a procedure that involves painting a cortisone solution on the skin and then driving it into the tendon using an electric current. Some exciting new developments in highly specialized injection techniques may also aid in the healing process of damaged tendons.

In rare cases, surgery is necessary to repair tennis elbow. This is usually required only when the tendon has actually detached from the bone.

Typically, athletes with tennis elbow can return to play as soon as they can comfortably practice and play their sports. If your doctor prescribes a tennis elbow brace that takes away your pain effectively, you may be able to return to play even sooner.

LITTLE LEAGUE ELBOW

Little League elbow describes a group of elbow problems related to the stress of pitching and throwing in young athletes.

The growth plates of the elbow close at about age 14 to 16. Until then, teen athletes—particularly pitchers who throw too often and too hard—are at risk for Little League elbow. Infielders, catchers, and outfielders can also develop Little League elbow, as can athletes who participate in other overhead throwing sports such as tennis and football. The repeated throwing motion causes irritation on the growth plates at the end of the forearm bones in the elbow joint. Because the bones are growing faster than the tendons, the attachment site, called the growth center or apophysis, becomes stressed at the medial epicondyle. Over time, the constant yanking of the wrist flexors caused by pitching pulls this growth center apart, which leads to pain and inflammation in the elbow.

In addition to pain, Little League elbow can make it difficult to fully extend your elbow. If you're a younger baseball or softball player—particularly if you are a pitcher—and you have symptoms of Little League elbow, see your doctor. If the diagnosis is indeed Little League elbow, the treatment will be rest (no throwing)—anywhere from a few weeks to six months, depending on the severity of your injury, as well as ice and nonsteroidal anti-inflammatory medications.

The best treatment for Little League elbow, however, is to prevent if from ever developing in the first place. In severe cases, Little League elbow can cause a separation of the bone at the attachment, leading to severe pain and restricted arm motion. This is a medical emergency that requires surgery and months of physical rehabilitation. In some rare cases, this injury can end a pitching career.

To help prevent Little League elbow, limit the number of pitches you throw. Some Little Leagues restrict the number of innings pitchers can throw per week. But if your Little League isn't regulated or if you play on a high school team, you will have to keep track yourself. You and your coach should limit the number of weekly pitches to no more than 80 twice a week. (It's the number of throws—not the number of innings—that makes the biggest difference.)

If your high school or Little League coach is putting you in for long stretches of every game and you're starting to develop some discomfort in your elbow, speak up. Many coaches aren't familiar with Little League elbow, and they don't realize that overuse can cause the condition. Another effective way to prevent Little League elbow is to make sure you are throwing properly. If you're not sure, ask your school trainer to evaluate your form.

In most cases, athletes with Little League elbow can return to the field as soon as they can practice and play comfortably.

GOLFER'S ELBOW

In teenagers who hit the course frequently—either as part of the high school golf team or recreationally on the weekends—golfer's elbow can strike. Golfer's elbow, also known as medial epicondylitis, is pain and inflammation on the inner side of the elbow, where the tendons of the forearm muscles attach to the bump on the inside of the elbow.

In addition to golf, tennis, other racquet sports, throwing sports, and other activities such as painting, raking leaves, chopping wood, and typing can cause golfer's elbow. Golfer's elbow (sometimes referred to as "medial tennis elbow") is rather common in more advanced tennis players who impart a lot of topspin by using their wrist.

Symptoms of golfer's elbow include inner elbow pain, pain that radiates into the forearm and wrist, stiffness in the elbow, weakness in the hands and wrists, or tingling that radiates to the fingers. The pain of golfer's elbow may get worse when you shake hands, turn a doorknob, squeeze or pitch a ball, swing a golf club or tennis racquet, or pick up an object with your palm facing down.

If you are experiencing symptoms of golfer's elbow, you can start by resting your elbow, icing it on and off for 15 to 20 minutes, and taking over-the-counter pain relievers. You can also try wearing an elbow brace similar to a tennis elbow brace, but positioned on the inner instead of the outer elbow. If the pain doesn't ease in a few days, see your doctor.

To diagnose golfer's elbow, your doctor will perform a physical exam and possibly order an X-ray to rule out other causes of your pain, such as arthritis or an elbow fracture.

To help speed healing, in addition to RICE and NSAIDS, your doctor may suggest specific exercises to strengthen and stretch your elbow. In severe cases, surgery may be required.

You will be able to get back on the course or court following golfer's elbow once the pain is gone and you have regained full range of motion. You may want to review your golf or tennis swing with a physical therapist or your school's trainer to help prevent reinjury.

ULNAR COLLATERAL LIGAMENT INJURIES

The *ulnar collateral ligament* (UCL) is a ligament that helps stabilize the elbow. It is composed of three bands—the anterior, posterior, and transverse bands—and it spans from the ulna (a bone in the forearm) to the humerus (the bone of the upper arm). The UCL is subject to injury when stress is placed on the elbow during throwing and other activities. The UCL is particularly vulnerable to injury in athletes who have biomechanical problems, weaknesses, or restrictions anywhere in the kinetic chain from the hips through the shoulders involved in the throwing motion.

Over time, stress on the elbow causes microscopic tears in the UCL. This stress causes the ligament to stretch out, so it no longer holds the bones of the elbow together tightly enough during throwing motions.

The UCL can also be injured suddenly, during a particular throw. In this case, the athlete may notice a sharp "pop" or develop sudden severe pain on the inside of the elbow while throwing.

UCL injuries tend to mimic the symptoms of Little League elbow, but they are more common in older teenage athletes. Symptoms of a UCL tear include pain in the elbow felt during the phase of throwing when the arm accelerates forward, and irritation of the ulnar nerve (funny bone nerve). While someone with a UCL tear may notice the pain when he or she throws, everyday activities, such as carrying a bag of groceries won't necessarily cause pain.

If your symptoms point to a UCL tear, see your doctor. He or she will perform a physical examination and possibly order an X-ray or MRI to take a closer look at your elbow. The initial treatment for a UCL tear includes rest, ice on and off to reduce swelling, and NSAIDS. Your doctor may also prescribe exercises or physical therapy to strengthen the muscles around the elbow.

The type of treatment that follows will depend on an athlete's individual goals. If you simply want to reduce your pain and make your elbow joint more stable, you will probably not need surgery. If you wish to return to strenuous throwing activities, however, surgery may be in order. There are also currently some nonsurgical procedures (injections) that can help strengthen ligaments; these are investigational at this point and may be considered on a case-by-case basis. You will need to discuss the pros and cons of surgery with your doctor.

Return to play following a UCL tear will depend on the individual injury and the course of treatment.

TRICEPS TENDONITIS

When you throw a ball, your elbow starts in the bent position and straightens out as the ball leaves your hand. This sudden bending motion can stress the area of your elbow where your triceps tendon attaches to the elbow joint, causing triceps tendonitis. Sports that involve repeated throwing, such as baseball and softball, can lead to triceps tendonitis.

Symptoms of triceps tendonitis include severe pain on the back of your elbow, right above the elbow joint, where the triceps tendon hooks to the back of the elbow. Pain is likely to worsen when you perform activities that involve loaded elbow extension such as push-ups, bench presses, or triceps extensions. This pain tends to be particularly severe in baseball pitchers. You may also feel a snapping sensation in your elbow.

If you experience pain above your elbow joint and you participate in a sport that involves throwing, see your doctor. He or she will confirm the diagnosis of triceps tendonitis and prescribe strengthening exercises for you. Other treatment options include rest, ice, NSAIDS, and a tennis elbow brace positioned on the back of your elbow, just above your elbow joint.

In severe cases, triceps tendonitis doesn't respond to strengthening exercises and requires a cortisone shot in the triceps tendon to decrease the pain and inflammation. If this is the case, performing strengthening exercises after the shot will help speed healing and prevent reinjury to the area.

BICEPS TENDONITIS

If you have pain in the lower part of your biceps muscle close to your elbow on the front of the elbow joint, you could be suffering from biceps tendonitis. Common in beginning weight lifters who lift too much weight too fast (especially lifters who perform biceps curls or prayer curls), biceps tendonitis usually leads to severe pain the day *after* lifting. Other symptoms include not being able to fully extend your elbow due to the swelling and spasms in the overstressed biceps muscle fibers. In some cases, the pain is so severe and the range of motion is so restricted that the sufferer can't raise a fork to his or her mouth to eat.

The treatment for biceps tendonitis involves resting the elbow and icing the area for 20 minutes at a time, three to four times a day for the first two days following the injury. If you notice some improvement after the first two days, you can start a gentle stretching program to help relax and lengthen the muscle fibers so you can completely bend your elbow once again. During this time, you should try to carefully straighten your elbow often to restore your full range of motion. Try to do this on and off for three or four days. You should be able to return to play once you have full range of motion and strength in your elbow.

PITCHER'S ELBOW
(OSTEOCHONDRITIS DESSICANS)

When pitchers throw the ball, they go through a series of stages, requiring the elbow to bend up to 100 degrees.

Pitcher's elbow tends to affect athletes who snap their wrists downward and inward as part of the motions required by their sports. For example, when a pitcher pitches, there is a strong external rotational force placed on the elbow that can compress the outer side. This force causes the ligaments that hold the inner bones of the elbow together—the flexor muscles—to stretch and become inflamed and painful. Concurrently, the compression of the outer side of the elbow causes the head of the outer forearm bone (the radius) to push against the upper arm bone (the humerus). In addition to pitchers, golfers, rowers, and tennis players are also at risk for this injury.

Over time, this compression in the elbow can cause part of the bone in the humerus to die. The dead piece of bone can fall into the elbow joint, leaving a hole where it used to be. This hole leads to pain and a "clicking" sensation when the elbow moves. If the piece of bone gets stuck in the joint, the elbow can lock. This injury is known as pitcher's elbow, or osteochondritis dessicans.

If you experience pain and clicking in your elbow, see your doctor. He or she will perform a physical examination and some tests to determine if you indeed have pitcher's elbow.

Because the main cause of pitcher's elbow is throwing too many pitches, the primary treatment is rest to allow the ligament and bone in your elbow to heal. In severe cases, surgery may also be required.

After your elbow heals, your doctor will ask you to throw fewer pitches and to change your pitching routine (with the help of your doctor or school trainer), so you don't reinjure the area.

POPEYE ELBOW

Named for the large-armed spinach-loving character himself, Popeye elbow (or olecranon *bursitis*) refers not to Popeye's huge forearms but to the tiny knobs he had sticking out from behind his elbows. When the bursal sac called the olecranon bursa becomes inflamed, it leads to bursitis in the elbow. You may develop this injury if you lean excessively on your elbows (for example, while talking on the phone) or are hit on the end of your elbow during sports practice or play.

Symptoms of Popeye elbow include a noticeable bump on the back of the elbow and pain and inflammation in the area that results from the irritated bursal sac. There is often little or no pain with Popeye elbow, however. In the case of chronic Popeye elbow, you may feel little bumps behind your elbow when you move it. Although they are sometimes misdiagnosed as bone chips, these lumps are actually a thickening in the wall of the bursal sac that results from constant inflammation.

If Popeye elbow develops suddenly as a result of a blow to the elbow, treatment will involve draining the excess fluid in the bursal sac with a needle, occasionally followed by a cortisone injection. Following drainage, your doctor will likely apply compression, which is important to maintain for a couple of days in order to prevent the fluid from building again.

There isn't much you can do to prevent acute Popeye elbow other than to use elbow pads during sports for protection. If the condition is chronic, on the other hand, try to avoid leaning on your elbows.

HYPEREXTENSION INJURIES

When a blow to your elbow causes it to bend too far the wrong way, it leads to *hyperextension*. The elbow extends farther than normal, resulting in a tear of the fibers that join the front of the elbow joint. At the same time, it overextends the biceps muscle that attaches just below the elbow. Sports that tend to lead to hyperextension injuries of the elbow include wrestling, gymnastics, football, and some throwing sports.

Symptoms of a hyperextended elbow include pain and swelling in the elbow joint. If you know you've hyperextended your elbow, you may be able to treat this injury on your own with rest and ice.

If the pain and swelling persist for more than a few days, however, see your doctor. He or she may prescribe a splint you can wear to keep your elbow joint in the proper position until it has fully healed. When the splint comes off, you will have to gently stretch your elbow until you can fully extend your arm without any pain or discomfort.

Once the pain of a hyperextended elbow has subsided—whether you have treated it yourself or with the help of your doctor—you can begin to strengthen your elbow with arm curls using light dumbbells. Depending on the extent of the injury, you should be able to return to play in about three to six weeks.

ELBOW DISLOCATION

Elbow dislocations usually result from a fall or a twisting injury to the elbow. If you fall on an outstretched arm and have severe pain and an obvious deformity in your elbow, you most likely have an elbow dislocation.

If you suspect an elbow dislocation, seek medical attention. In the meantime, immobilize your elbow in the position it took after you injured it; do not attempt to put it back in place yourself.

To treat an elbow dislocation, your physician will reduce it (put it back in place) after putting you to sleep. Following the reduction, you will probably wear a splint to immobilize your elbow for seven to 10 days. Your doctor may also prescribe gentle range-of-motion exercises at this point. Once the splint comes off, you will most likely wear a sling for an additional two to three weeks. After three to five weeks, you will be able to perform some light flexion and extension exercises to improve your range of motion.

ELBOW FRACTURE

An elbow fracture is a break that involves one or more of the three bones that work together to form the elbow joint. If you suffer a trauma to your elbow, such as a fall on an outstretched arm or a blow to your elbow and severe elbow pain follows, you may have sustained an elbow fracture.

What's the Difference between Little League Elbow, Golfer's Elbow, and Tennis Elbow?

The elbow is not a large joint, so it can be difficult to tell if pain there is due to tennis elbow, golfer's elbow, Little League elbow, or another elbow injury. Here are some tips on how to tell the difference:

▸ Tennis elbow leads to pain on the outside of the elbow and gets worse when you apply pressure to the area or try to lift things with your palm facing down.

▸ Tennis elbow is usually aggravated when you try to extend your wrist or middle finger against resistance. You can try to do this as a self-test.

▸ Golfer's elbow is similar to tennis elbow, but the injury occurs on the inside rather than the outside of the elbow.

▸ Golfer's elbow leads to pain that radiates into the forearm and wrist, stiffness in the elbow, weakness in the hands and wrists, or rarely, tingling that radiates to the fingers.

▸ The pain of golfer's elbow may get worse when you shake hands, turn a doorknob, squeeze or pitch a ball, or swing a golf club or tennis racquet.

▸ Golfer's elbow pain may also get worse when you shake hands or try to lift something with the palm facing upward.

▸ Little League elbow is difficult to differentiate from golfer's elbow because the two injuries are connected. However, you will notice symptoms of Little League elbow, which include pain and swelling on the inside of the elbow, during/after pitching or throwing.

▸ Someone suffering from Little League elbow will complain of pain and swelling on the inside of the elbow that came on after pitching for an extended period of time.

Symptoms of an elbow fracture include swelling on your elbow or just above it, deformity in your elbow, redness or bruising, numbness or a cool sensation in your forearm, hand, or fingers, a tight sensation in your forearm or elbow, and/or difficulty moving your elbow joint.

To determine if you have fractured your elbow, try to extend your elbow fully (so your arm is completely outstretched in front of you) with your palm facing upward. If you can do this, an elbow fracture is unlikely.

If you cannot perform the above motion and you suspect an elbow fracture, seek medical attention immediately. Elbow fractures that go untreated can lead to permanent loss of function or arthritis in the joint.

To diagnose an elbow fracture, your doctor will perform a physical examination and order X-rays. Treatment will depend on the extent of your injury. In the case of a milder fracture (for instance, a nondisplaced radial head fracture), you may have to wear a splint, apply ice to decrease swelling, and take pain relievers. If the fracture is more severe, treatment may include surgery to repair the broken bones, blood vessels, and/or nerves in your elbow and forearm.

TORN BICEPS

Although it's rare, teenage athletes have been known to tear biceps muscles. Biceps tears usually result from a sudden severe movement of the arm that causes the biceps muscle to literally tear in half. A tennis player who hits a hard forearm shot, a golfer who accidentally hits the ground hard with his or her club, or a weight lifter who lifts too much weight too fast are all vulnerable to a torn biceps muscle.

Symptoms of a biceps tear include pain, loss of function, bleeding, and a visual deformity. If you experience a sudden jerking motion in your elbow and you suspect you have torn your biceps, seek medical attention.

Treatment of a biceps tear involves resting the torn muscle for two to three weeks and then strengthening the other head of the biceps muscle to help it take over full function while the injured head heals. Unfortunately, once you tear a biceps muscle, it never completely returns to normal. Cosmetic surgery may help correct the visual defect, but it may not fully restore the original strength in the muscle. Once you tear a biceps muscle, you are also more likely to tear it again.

PREVENTING ELBOW INJURIES

As mentioned in some of the injuries above, throwing and/or pitching are common causes of elbow injuries in teenage athletes. These injuries are particularly prevalent in pitchers who throw too many pitches too often. Training errors such as abrupt changes in the frequency, intensity, or duration of throwing activity are also associated with elbow injuries, as are poor coaching and lack of preseason conditioning. Therefore, if you participate in a pitching or throwing sport, limiting your number of throws and the intensity at which you throw can help prevent elbow injuries, as can making sure you are properly trained and conditioned when your sports season starts.

Exercises that strengthen the elbow and improve flexibility of the joint can also do a lot in the prevention of both acute and chronic injuries to the area. Since imbalances in strength and flexibility in the entire upper extremity, including the shoulders, trunk, hips, etc. can put the elbow at risk for injury, exercises that strengthen and improve flexibility in these areas can also go far in the prevention of elbow injuries.

In addition, the following actions can help prevent elbow injuries:

➤ Make sure you have proper footwear and level playing surfaces; this can help to prevent some of the imbalances that can lead to improper throwing form and, therefore, elbow injuries.
➤ Work on your form. If you play a sport that puts you at risk for elbow injuries, ask your school trainer to analyze your form. Sometimes problems with your swing or throw can overload the muscles in your elbow or wrist, leading to injury.
➤ Lift weights wisely. Don't lift too much weight too fast, and keep your wrist stable to reduce the force transmitted to your elbows.
➤ Rest. As soon as you feel elbow pain, stop the activity that is causing it and take a break for a few days. Sometimes taking just a few days off can prevent an injury that could take you out of your sport for weeks or months.

EXERCISES THAT HELP PREVENT AND TREAT ELBOW INJURIES

Wrist curl. Standing with your feet shoulder-width apart, hold a dumbbell with your arm down by your side and your elbow locked. With your palm facing forward, flex your wrist forward all the way, then let it back down. Repeat this exercise 50 times or until your muscle is exhausted. Then switch sides.

Reverse wrist curl. Standing with your feet shoulder-width apart, hold a dumbbell with your arm down by your side and turn your hand so your palm faces backward. Flex your wrist forward as far as it will go, then let it down. Repeat 50 times or to the point of your muscle exhaustion. Then switch sides.

Ball squeeze. Hold a soft rubber ball or a tennis ball and squeeze it continually until your hand is fatigued.

Triceps curl. Hold a dumbbell in one hand. Lift the dumbbell up over your shoulder and then drop it back behind your head. Place your opposite hand between your shoulder and your elbow to help hold your arm up. Raise the dumbbell straight over your head, working your triceps muscle. Then slowly drop the dumbbell behind your head once again.

Biceps stretch. Grasp the underside of a heavy object, such as a table or countertop. Gently pull yourself backward so that your elbow straightens out. Pull on the object until you feel a strain in the muscle just above your elbow and hold for 20 to 30 seconds. Repeat with the other side.

Elbow stretch. Extend your right arm with your elbow locked and your palm facing down so your arm is parallel to the floor. Push the top of your hand and fingers of the extended hand down toward the floor with your other hand as far as they will go and hold for 15 to 20 seconds. Repeat with the other side.

Pronation using resistance band. Tie one end of a resistance band around something sturdy at waist height, such as a doorknob, with the arm that you plan to work first closest to the attachment point. Wrap the other end of the resistance band around the end of a long, thin object and hold the other end. Bend your elbow and hold your upper arm against your side. Start with your hand positioned so your thumb faces up, then turn your hand over so that the palm faces down (pronate). Return to the starting position.

Supination using resistance band. Tie one end of a resistance band around something sturdy at waist height, such as a doorknob, with the arm that you plan to work first closest to the attachment point. Wrap the other end of the resistance band around the end of a long, thin object and hold the other end. Bend your elbow and hold your upper arm against your side. Start with your hand positioned so your thumb faces down, then turn your hand over so that the palm faces up (supinate). Return to the starting position.

WHAT YOU NEED TO KNOW

- ▶ Because the elbow is still forming in the teenage years, you are more at risk for elbow injuries as a teen athlete.
- ▶ Chronic elbow injuries can usually be self-treated in the short term with RICE and NSAIDS.
- ▶ When it comes to chronic elbow injuries, the most effective treatment is often addressing the biomechanical errors that led to the injury in the first place.
- ▶ Acute elbow injuries tend to result from a fall on an out-stretched arm.
- ▶ If you experience a sudden elbow injury that leads to severe pain, swelling, or an inability to move your elbow, seek medical attention immediately. In the meantime, splint the injured arm, secure it with an elastic wrap, and apply ice to the area in 10- to 20-minute intervals until help arrives.
- ▶ No matter if it is acute or chronic, do not take an elbow injury lightly; left untreated, some elbow injuries can limit sports play, lead to other injuries, or cause permanent problems.
- ▶ To help prevent elbow injuries, do the following:
  - If you participate in pitching or throwing as part of your sport, limit your number of weekly throws.
  - Perform exercises that strengthen your elbow and improve flexibility in the joint.
  - Since imbalances in strength and flexibility in the entire upper extremity can lead to elbow injury, perform exercises that improve strength and flexibility in your shoulders, trunk, hips, etc.
  - Make sure you have the proper footwear and a level playing surface.
  - Ask your school trainer to evaluate your throwing form.
  - Lift weights wisely. Don't lift too much weight too fast, and keep your wrists stable.
  - Rest as soon as you feel elbow pain.

6

Wrist and Hand Injuries

Harry, 18, is one of the best wrestlers on his varsity high school team. During his last meet, Harry was unexpectedly pinned by an opponent he thought he'd beat. As he walked out of the gym after his defeat, Harry took out his frustration the wrong way—he punched the wall. As soon as his fist hit the concrete, Harry knew he'd broken his hand.

When Harry arrived at the emergency room, the doctors confirmed the fracture in his hand and diagnosed him with a *boxer's fracture.* Now Harry can't wrestle for the rest of the season. And although his fracture wasn't the direct result of his sport, Harry learned a hard lesson about sportsmanship.

INTRODUCTION TO WRIST AND HAND INJURIES

Despite the small space they take up, the wrist and hand are some of the most complex—and important—structures on the human body. Many injuries to the wrist and hand are obvious, but some are more subtle, requiring a more detailed examination for diagnosis.

Injuries to the wrist and hand are common in teen athletes. Many wrist and hand injuries are caused by a fall on an outstretched hand, and teenagers—while playing sports and in their everyday activities—are more likely than adults to use their arms and hands to try to break a fall.

This chapter will cover some of the most common injuries of the wrist and hand and offer tips on how teen athletes can best prevent and treat these injuries. Some of the specific injuries covered will include collateral ligament injuries (*skier's thumb* and gamekeeper's thumb), wrist sprains, wrist fractures, boxer's fractures (fractures of the metacarpal), and finger injuries.

THE WRIST

The wrist comprises 10 bones that help it move in different directions (eight small hand bones, called carpal bones, and two long bones in the forearm—the radius and the ulna). These 10 bones allow you to bend, straighten, and rotate your wrist so you can pitch a ball, swing a hammer, or jump rope. These wrist bones are quite brittle, and, therefore, sensitive to excessive force or trauma.

To help the hand and fingers move, flexor and extensor tendons cross the wrist, along with the ulnar, median, and radial nerves.

Sports that typically lead to wrist injuries include racquet and throwing sports, which require the athlete to snap his or her wrist. The forceful motions in football, boxing, gymnastics, and wrestling, where the wrist is used to grasp and pull, can also lead to wrist injuries. Adventure sports such as snowboarding and skiing tend to lead to injuries in the wrist area as well.

SPRAINED WRIST

With all you ask of your wrist, unfortunately, there are few muscles in the wrist to stabilize it. As a result, the ligaments that interconnect the bones in the wrist are vulnerable to being sprained, particularly if you play sports.

Wrist sprains range in severity from a stretching of the ligaments (simple sprain) to partial and complete tears, which can lead to wrist instability and dislocation. The most commonly injured ligament in the wrist is called the scapholunate ligament.

In the case of a simple sprain, the supporting ligaments on the radiocarpal joint in the wrist become stretched, most often as a result of a fall on an extended wrist. Simple sprains usually lead to mild pain and stiffness in the wrist without affecting range of motion. If your doctor takes an X-ray of a simple sprain, it will appear normal.

The most serious wrist sprain is a subluxation of the wrist bones, which occurs when the ligaments connecting two or more of the small bones in the wrist are completely torn, causing the bones to become displaced. This sprain is most common in boxers, but teens who play certain sports or who, like Harry, have a bit of a temper, are also at risk.

If you sustain an injury to your wrist and you suspect a sprain, see your doctor if the pain doesn't go away in a day or two. A sprained wrist may lead to long-term or even permanent problems. For example, the sprained ligament may allow bones to become unstable, or in some cases pull off a small piece of bone, making the injury fracture as well.

Treatment for a sprained wrist typically includes over-the-counter pain relievers such as ibuprofen (Advil, Motrin), acetaminophen (Tylenol), or naproxen sodium (Aleve), rest, ice, and immobilization, followed by exercises to improve flexibility and strength. In severe cases, surgery may be required.

BROKEN WRIST

Fractures are one of the most common sports-related wrist injuries in teenagers. In children and teens, the growing bones in the wrist are more susceptible to stress and, therefore, fractures than the ligaments that surround them.

Often the result of a fall or blow, some wrist fractures are initially written off as a sprain; the athlete thinks he or she has a wrist sprain that won't heal, when actually he or she has a broken wrist.

It's possible to break any bone in your wrist, but the bones most vulnerable to fractures are the two in the forearm that lead to the wrist—the radius and the ulna. Radius fractures, also called distal radius fractures or Colles' fractures, account for an estimated 35 to 47 percent of wrist fractures and usually result from a ski accident or a fall on an outstretched hand.

Another commonly broken wrist bone is the scaphoid bone (also called the navicular bone), which is located in the wrist, just behind the base of your thumb. This type of fracture is usually caused by falling on an outstretched arm (in an attempt to break the fall). Scaphoid fractures are hard to diagnose because (1) they don't always cause much pain, so the person suffering from one may not seek medical attention right away, and (2) they are often missed on X-rays. It's crucial that scaphoid fractures get properly diagnosed, however, because they can lead to permanent problems if they are left untreated.

All sports put you at risk for a wrist fracture, but the sports that make you most vulnerable include soccer, skiing, rugby, dancing, football, snowboarding, and ice skating.

No matter which bones have been broken, a wrist fracture will usually cause the following symptoms:

▸ Severe pain
▸ Numbness
▸ Swelling
▸ Trouble moving your fingers
▸ Decreased grip strength

If you suspect a wrist fracture, see your doctor. Untreated wrist fractures—particularly navicular fractures—can lead to loss of motion and chronic wrist pain.

To diagnose a broken wrist, your doctor will perform a physical examination to look for tenderness, deformity, and swelling, and order an X-ray, CT scan, or MRI.

Treatment for a wrist fracture first involves immobilization; keeping the bone still is crucial to proper healing. Beyond immobilization, treatment will depend on the severity and type of the fracture. If your wrist has been displaced, your doctor may need to perform a reduction (which means putting the displaced bones back into their proper places). Whether or not a reduction is necessary, your doctor will probably send you home in a splint and tell you to rest and ice the fracture until you can visit an orthopedic specialist, who will evaluate your injury to see if further treatment is necessary. In the case of severe wrist fractures, surgery may be necessary to stabilize the wrist with wires, plates, nails, or screws.

In addition, your doctor may prescribe a prescription painkiller or instruct you to take an over-the-counter pain reliever such as ibuprofen (Advil, Motrin), acetaminophen (Tylenol), or naproxen sodium (Aleve). Be sure to ask your doctor before you take an over-the-counter pain reliever on your own for a fracture; some nonsteroidal anti-inflammatory medications (NSAIDS) may slow healing.

Unfortunately, wrist fractures often take longer than other fractures in the body to heal because the area may not get adequate blood supply. In some cases, they can take up to eight months to heal. To speed healing, your doctor may prescribe an electromagnetic device called a bone stimulator to use with your cast. If the bones do not heal properly in a cast, you may need surgery to correct a broken wrist.

Rehabilitation may help to speed healing of a broken wrist. In most cases, your doctor will instruct you to perform at least some sort of motion to minimize stiffness in your wrist while it is immobilized in a splint or cast.

Once the splint or cast is removed, your doctor may prescribe additional exercises to help restore movement and decrease stiffness in your wrist. Keep in mind that it can take several months to restore full range of motion following a wrist fracture.

TENDONITIS

Like a bridge, the wrist acts as a passageway for tendons that extend from the fingers to the forearm. In fact, your fingers are actually controlled largely by muscles in your forearm versus your hand. In some sports, overuse of the wrist can lead to tendonitis—an inflammation of these finger-to-forearm tendons, leading to swelling, pain, and loss of function in one or more of the fingers.

Two wrist tendons are particularly vulnerable to tendonitis—the flexor and extensor tendons in the thumb that help the thumb move toward and away from the pointer finger. This type of tendonitis leads to swelling and pain on the thumb side of the wrist. In tennis players, it is often due to a hard racquet grip.

If you suspect you have tendonitis in your wrist, see your doctor. Treatment involves rest and ice initially, followed by immobilization and either prescription or over-the-counter anti-inflammatory medications. Your doctor may also prescribe a thumb splint or cortisone injections as part of your treatment.

After the tendonitis has subsided, you can perform exercises to strengthen the muscles and tendons in your wrist to prevent them from becoming overstressed once again.

WRIST CARTILAGE

On the side of your wrist that aligns with the pinky, where the ulna meets the wrist, there is a cartilage complex called the triangular fibrocartilage complex (TFCC). This structure, much like the *meniscus* in the knee or the *labrum* in the shoulder, may tear when subjected to excessive force. Certain people, by virtue of the shape of their wrist joint, are more vulnerable than others to injuries to this structure. TFCC tears often result in pain, clicking, or catching in this part of the wrist joint. Physical therapy is sometimes helpful, but surgery is often recommended to repair the tear if symptoms persist.

THE HAND

Not only are your hands crucial to good sports performance, they are also imperative to everyday activities. Therefore, any injury to your

---

Why Do So Many Teenagers Suffer Torus (Buckle) Fractures?

As a teenager, your bones are softer than those of your parents. Your bones are harder than they were when you were a kid, but they are still solidifying. Therefore, your bones are more vulnerable to certain types of fractures; one such fracture is called a torus fracture, or a "buckle fracture."

Torus fractures are a form of the most common type of wrist fracture—a distal radial fracture. Torus fractures result when one side of the bone bends, raising a little buckle, without breaking the other side. Because teens have softer bones, which are more likely to bend than break, these fractures are particularly common in young teenage athletes. Mature bones, on the other hand, are more likely to break completely.

Luckily, torus fractures usually don't require a reduction, and they tend to heal well with rest and immobilization. Because teenagers' bones are still growing, they heal faster.

---

hand(s)—even if it is just a finger—should be seen by a doctor. In many cases, hand injuries are best treated by a hand surgeon rather than a general orthopedist. The physician at the emergency room or your primary care physician can help you to determine the best course of action for you.

Because your hands are so important, if you injure one or both of them, you should seek a specialist for rehabilitative therapy. A physical therapist who specializes in hand injuries will be able to prescribe exercises you can perform to improve the flexibility, strength, and range of motion in your hands.

Here are some of the more common hand injuries in teenage athletes:

BROKEN HAND

Although broken hands are usually caused by an angry person who punches a wall, they can also result from a football player smashing his hand into another player's helmet by accident, one player stepping on another player's hand, a fall during a gymnastics routine, and other sports mishaps.

With all the metacarpals (hand bones) and the phalanges (finger bones), there are many bones in the hand and, therefore, many different types of hand fractures. The metacarpals, which are longer bones, are rather vulnerable to being broken, and they may at times be problematic if not treated properly.

Symptoms of a broken hand include the following:

- Severe pain
- Numbness
- Swelling
- Bruising in the hand
- Trouble moving your fingers
- Deformity or malalignment of the fingers, especially when making a fist

If you injure your hand during sports play and you have any reason to suspect a fracture, seek medical attention right away. A broken hand is an emergency, and if it isn't treated in time, it can lead to poor healing, weakened grip strength, and decreased range of motion.

To diagnose a broken hand, your doctor will perform a physical examination to look for tenderness, deformity, and swelling, and order an X-ray, CT scan, or MRI. Because there are so many different bones in the hand, there are numerous different types of hand fractures; your doctor will be able to determine the type of fracture you have suffered and, therefore, the best course of treatment.

If a fracture is confirmed, treatment will most likely first require immobilization. Keeping the bone(s) still is crucial to proper healing. Beyond immobilization, treatment will depend on the severity and type of the fracture. If the broken bone has been displaced, your doctor may need to perform a reduction (which means putting these bones back into their proper places). Whether or not a reduction is necessary, your doctor will probably send you home in a splint or cast, which you will wear for three to eight weeks. Depending on the location of the break, you may be able to get by with a light plastic splint for only a few weeks, which will allow you to return to play much sooner.

In addition, your doctor may prescribe a prescription painkiller or instruct you to take an over-the-counter pain reliever such as ibuprofen (Advil, Motrin), acetaminophen (Tylenol), or naproxen sodium (Aleve). Be sure to ask your doctor before you take an over-the-counter pain reliever on your own for a fracture; some nonsteroidal anti-inflammatory medications (NSAIDS) may actually slow healing.

Your doctor may also send you to an orthopedic specialist, who will evaluate your injury to see if further treatment is necessary. In the case of severe hand fractures, surgery may be necessary.

Physical therapy may help to speed healing of a broken hand. In most cases, your doctor will instruct you to perform at least some sort of motion to minimize stiffness while your hand is immobilized in a splint or cast.

Once the splint or cast is removed, your doctor may prescribe additional exercises to help restore movement and decrease stiffness. Keep in mind that it can take several months to restore full range of motion following a hand fracture.

BOXER'S FRACTURE

One common type of hand fracture in teens is boxer's fracture. Just as the name implies, a boxer's fracture is a punching injury that affects the bones leading to your little finger, called the metacarpal bones. More specifically, it is a break of the bones of the hand that form the knuckles.

Boxer's fractures typically result from punching an object with a closed fist. That object may be a person or a wall. Boxer's fractures can also occur when an unclenched hand strikes a hard object.

There are five metacarpal bones in the hand, one to connect each finger to the wrist. Each bone has a base, shaft, neck, and head. The base is the portion of the bone that attaches to the wrist. The shaft is the long, slender portion of the bone. The neck is the part of the bone that connects the shaft to the head, and the head (or the knuckle) connects the metacarpal bone to the finger bone.

Boxer's fractures typically occur in the fourth and fifth metacarpal bones, which connect the ring and little fingers to the wrist respectively, most frequently in the fifth metacarpal. In addition, some doctors will classify breaks in the necks of the second and third metacarpal bones under the term *boxer's fracture* as well. These bones connect the index and middle fingers to the wrist.

Symptoms of a boxer's fracture include pain or tenderness around one or more knuckles. The pain may get worse when you move your hand or fingers. Other symptoms may include:

▸ A popping or snapping sensation when the bone breaks
▸ Swelling, discoloration, or bruising on the affected hand
▸ Decreased ability to move the hand

> ▸ Deformity of the broken bone or the knuckle
> ▸ Misalignment of the associated finger
> ▸ A cut on the hand (typically associated with a severe boxer's fracture)

If you think you may have sustained a boxer's fracture, see your doctor. If your doctor isn't available, seek emergency medical care. In the meantime, apply ice on and off to help keep the swelling down.

Once you arrive at your doctor's office or hospital, the doctor will look for the above signs and symptoms, perform a physical examination, and possibly conduct an X-ray to confirm the diagnosis.

Treatment for boxer's fracture will depend on the severity of the injury, but it will include some form of immobilization and pain relief. Your doctor will most likely prescribe a splint that extends from the fingers (with the fingers exposed) to the forearm near the elbow. He or she may also tape your ring and little fingers together.

To help ease the pain, your doctor may prescribe pain medication or instruct you to take over-the-counter painkillers such as acetaminophen (Tylenol) or ibuprofen (Advil).

In severe cases, surgery may be necessary to treat boxer's fracture. In this case, your doctor will most likely send you to a hand specialist for the surgery.

The best way to prevent a boxer's fracture is to avoid the situation that causes it; in short, don't punch anything. You can also help build stronger bones by engaging in regular exercise and increasing your intake of dairy products and other calcium-rich foods.

BROKEN FINGER

Any trauma to the finger can cause the bone to break. This commonly occurs while jamming your finger as you attempt to catch a ball, or having your finger bent by another individual (as in wrestling). It is often difficult to tell the difference between a sprained finger and a broken finger, and many times the treatment is the same or similar for both. When the break involves a joint, it may be a bit more problematic when it comes to regaining normal motion.

ULNAR COLLATERAL LIGAMENT INJURY

First coined in 1955 because it affected Scottish gamekeepers when they sacrificed game by breaking the animals' necks between the ground and their thumb and index fingers, gamekeeper's thumb (or skier's thumb) affects the ulnar collateral ligament (UCL, not to be confused with the ligament in the elbow with the same name), a band of tough, fibrous tissue that connects the bones at the base of the thumb and prevents the thumb from pointing too far away from the hand. When the UCL becomes injured or torn, the first metacarpophalangeal (MCP) joint—the joint that helps the thumb flex and extend—becomes unstable, making it difficult for the sufferer to grasp an object or pinch.

Today, people who suffer from gamekeeper's thumb don't usually get it by sacrificing animals, but rather by a fall during sports or everyday activity. Although the terms *gamekeeper's thumb* and *skier's thumb* are used interchangeably, they are slightly different. In general, skier's thumb is usually an acute injury caused by a fall (usually when a skier gets his or her hand stuck in the ski pole while falling). Gamekeeper's thumb, on the other hand, is usually caused by a chronic pattern of injury that gradually loosens the ligament over time. For the sake of diagnosis and treatment, however, these injuries are practically the same.

Although UCL injuries are most common in skiers, teen athletes who perform other sports can also suffer from them. For instance, a football player may suffer a UCL injury while making a tackle, falling on an outstretched hand, or over time by stressing the thumb while blocking. In addition, UCL injuries are common among athletes who handle balls (basketball, baseball, soccer, and football), as well as among those who carry sticks (hockey, lacrosse, etc.), because the balls and sticks can abduct the thumb during activity.

In addition to pain and swelling on the inner side of the thumb at the base, the most classic symptom of skier's thumb or gamekeeper's thumb is the inability to press the thumb sideways against the other fingers to grasp an object or to make a pinching motion. As an athlete, you may have trouble grasping a tennis racquet or throwing a baseball.

If you've suffered an injury to your thumb and you're having trouble picking things up, see your doctor right away. In the meantime, immobilize your thumb and apply ice to it on and off.

To diagnose skier's thumb or gamekeeper's thumb and determine the severity of the injury, your doctor will perform a physical examination to assess your ability to grip, grasp, and move your thumb. He or she may also order an X-ray, ultrasound, or MRI to rule out a fracture.

The goal of the treatment for UCL injuries is to help the ligaments heal so the thumb regains its full function. This treatment usually involves immobilization in a forearm cast or splint for about three to six weeks.

When the cast or splint comes off, your doctor will take a look at the injury and assess how well it has healed. If the swelling and tenderness have decreased and the joint appears to be stable, your doctor will most likely tell you to continue to wear a splint for two to four more weeks, taking it off several times a day to perform range-of-motion exercises in the joint.

In some cases, when immobilization doesn't sufficiently heal the ligament, or when the UCL has been completely torn, surgery may be necessary, especially if there is a resulting defect called a Stenar lesion. With a Stenar lesion, a piece of tissue gets in the way of the ligament trying to heal back to the bone. A splint is usually worn for four to five weeks following surgery. Athletes whose injuries require surgery can usually return to play in about three to four months.

After the period of immobilization is over, you will most likely perform exercises that help strengthen and stretch the joint so you can regain full function in your thumb.

Although there isn't much you can do to prevent skier's thumb, since it is usually an acute injury, one thing you can do is discard your ski poles if you fall while skiing.

OTHER FINGER INJURIES

Some of the most serious injuries to the wrist and hand are those that occur on the fingers. Many finger injuries are medical emergencies, and if they aren't treated properly and in time, they can lead to permanent problems.

If you suffer from a finger injury, you can make a homemade splint or "buddy tape" your injured finger to a neighboring finger to keep your finger still until you can get to the emergency room. To make a homemade splint, take a hard, flat object similar to the width of your finger and tape it against the injured part of your finger with medical tape. To "buddy tape" the finger, use medical tape to tape it against the finger next to it. Both of these techniques will help keep the finger immobilized until you can receive professional treatment.

Here are some of the more serious finger injuries that can occur in teenagers, as well as what you can do to recognize and treat them:

Jersey finger. A jersey finger, or a ruptured flexor tendon, is a serious finger injury that requires immediate attention. Jersey fingers usually result when one player's finger catches on another player's clothing during a tackling sport such as football or rugby. Symptoms include swelling and the inability to bend your finger. If you suffer a jersey finger, you should seek treatment immediately. You will be referred to an orthopedic or hand surgeon, who will probably perform surgery.

Mallet finger. As the name implies, mallet finger, or ruptured extensor tendon, is usually caused by an object (like a ball) striking the finger. Symptoms of mallet finger include pain at the top finger joint (called the dorsal DIP joint), inability to extend the dorsal DIP joint, and a finger deformity. Mallet finger is not as severe an injury as a jersey finger, but it must be splinted immediately and properly for about six weeks; without proper immobilization, you could be left with a permanent inability to fully straighten your finger.

Central slip rupture. A central slip extensor tendon injury occurs when the proximal interphalangeal (PIP) joint, the joint in the middle of your finger, is forcibly flexed during sports play. It is most common in basketball players. Symptoms include pain in the middle part of the finger and the inability to bend it. Treatment usually requires surgery. If you suspect a central slip rupture, seek medical attention immediately; if the injury isn't treated properly, a boutonniere deformity (where the top half of the finger becomes permanently straight and bent slightly downward) can develop within a few weeks.

Collateral ligament injury. This finger injury is commonly called a "jammed finger." The injury usually results from hitting something—like a basketball—head-on with your finger. Symptoms of a collateral ligament injury include swelling and a finger that appears to be displaced. If you suspect a collateral ligament injury, seek medical attention. Treatment will include immobilization in a splint for seven to 10 days. Your physician will most likely then "buddy tape" the injured finger to the finger next to it. It may take up to six months for a jammed finger to return to its normal size (in many cases, the joint remains permanently larger than the corresponding joint on the other hand), and a severe collateral ligament injury may permanently restrict finger motion.

Volar plate injury. If you hyperextend your finger (bend it backward too far), you can suffer a volar plate injury. The volar plate is a thick ligament on the metacarpophalangeal (MCP) joint of the finger, and it can be torn if the finger is hyperextended during sports play. Symptoms of a volar plate injury include tenderness in the finger. If you have hyperextended your finger and are experiencing pain, see your doctor as soon as possible. Treatment for a volar plate injury will depend on the severity. In more severe cases, your doctor may prescribe an aluminum splint. In less severe cases, he or she may "buddy tape" the injured finger to the finger next to it.

Pulley rupture. A common injury suffered while rock climbing, a pulley rupture is a tear of the pulley holding one or both of the tendons that help your fingers flex. Symptoms of a pulley rupture include a popping noise when the pulley ruptures (you may or may not hear this), pain, swelling, and possible bulging on the finger when it is flexed. If you suspect you've suffered a pulley rupture during climbing or a similar activity, see a hand surgeon as soon as possible. Depending on the severity of the rupture, treatment may include a splint or surgery to repair the damage. If left untreated, a pulley rupture can lead to further tears, arthritis, or a permanent loss of the ability to bend your finger.

PREVENTING WRIST AND HAND INJURIES

Although most wrist and hand injuries in sports occur as the result of accidents, there are a few things you can do to make a wrist or hand injury less likely. These basic tips may help you:

Use protective gear. If you are engaging in an activity that is high-risk for wrist and hand injuries, such as football, rugby, snowboarding, or skiing, wear wrist guards.

Don't dive into adventure sports. Planning to try snowboarding, surfing, inline skating, or another adventure sport that carries a high risk for wrist and hand injuries for the first time? Take it easy the first few times and consider professional instruction in order to decrease your risk of falls.

Wear the right shoes during sports play and in your everyday life. Falling onto an outstretched hand is the number-one cause of a broken hand or wrist. To decrease your risk of falling both during sports and in your everyday life, wear comfortable and supportive shoes or sneakers.

Bone up on calcium. A diet high in calcium-rich foods such as milk, cheese, and yogurt will help build strong bones and, therefore, prevent wrist and hand fractures. A high intake of calcium is particularly important for young women. Talk to your doctor about how much calcium you should eat per day, as well as the best ways to get more calcium into your diet.

STRETCHING AND STRENGTHENING EXERCISES FOR THE WRIST

Finger stretch. Starting with your right hand, gently extend each of your fingers as far back as they can go one by one, keeping them straight. Then pull all of your fingers back as far as they will go at the same time to stretch your palm. Then gently bring all your fingers forward as far as they will go (don't force them). Then make a fist and slowly open it, opening your fingers and thumb out as far as they will go.

Ball squeeze. Hold a soft foam ball or "stress ball" in your hand with your palm facing up. Squeeze the ball 15 to 20 times.

Rubber band opening. Place your finger tips inside a rubber band and try to stretch it open as far as possible, then release. Repeat 15 to 20 times.

Thumb walk. Holding your wrist straight, form the letter *o* with each finger by lightly touching your thumb to each fingertip. After each *o,* straighten and spread your fingers.

Door opener. Rest your forearm on a table, palm down. Keeping your little finger on the table, turn your hand so your palm faces up.

Wrist curl. Standing with your feet shoulder-width apart, hold a dumbbell with your arm down by your side and your elbow locked. With your palm facing forward, flex your wrist forward all the way and then let it back down. Repeat this exercise 50 times or until your muscle is exhausted. Then switch sides.

WHAT YOU NEED TO KNOW

> If you sustain an injury to your wrist and you suspect a sprain, see your doctor if the pain doesn't go away in a day or two. A sprained wrist may lead to long-term or even permanent problems.

> Often the result of a fall or blow, some wrist fractures are initially written off as a sprain; the athlete thinks he or she has a wrist sprain that won't heal, when actually, he or she has a broken wrist.

> No matter which bones have been broken, a wrist fracture usually causes severe pain, numbness, swelling, trouble moving your fingers, and decreased grip strength. If you suspect a wrist fracture, see your doctor.

➤ Be sure to ask your doctor before you take an over-the-counter pain reliever on your own for a fracture; some nonsteroidal anti-inflammatory medications (NSAIDS) may slow healing.

➤ In many cases, hand injuries are best treated by a hand surgeon rather than an orthopedist.

➤ If you injure your hand during sports play and you have any reason to suspect a fracture, seek medical attention right away. A broken hand is an emergency, and if it isn't treated in time, it can lead to poor healing, weakened grip strength, and decreased range of motion.

➤ Some of the most serious injuries to the wrist and hand are those that occur on the fingers. Many finger injuries are medical emergencies, and if they aren't treated properly and in time, they can lead to permanent problems.

➤ If you suffer from a finger injury, you can make a homemade splint or "buddy tape" your injured finger to a neighboring finger to keep your finger still until you can get to the emergency room.

7

Lower Back and Thorax Injuries

Maggie, 16, has been participating in gymnastics since she could walk. Now she's one of the best gymnasts on her high school team. A few weeks ago, Maggie started experiencing lower back pain during her floor routine. The pain got particularly strong when she extended her back during back handsprings and backbends.

When Maggie approached her coach about her lower back pain, he encouraged her to practice through it—after all, the state championships were coming up.

Maggie listened to her coach for a little while, but the pain grew worse. Frustrated and fearful of hurting herself more, Maggie made an appointment with her doctor. The diagnosis: *spondylolisthesis,* a stress fracture of part of the vertebrae that connect the front and rear portions of the bone that allows the vertebrae to slip out of place.

Depending on the severity, Maggie's diagnosis of spondylolisthesis may take her out of gymnastics for up to 12 months. Although she doesn't want to disappoint her coach, Maggie must now listen to her doctor and rest her back. In the meantime, she can do some light cardiovascular exercise to keep in shape, such as stationary cycling.

When it comes time to return to play, Maggie will have to work hard to get back to where she was preinjury. But she had no other option but to seek treatment for her pain.

Maggie's experience illustrates the importance of trusting your instincts and seeing a doctor when you have pain. Maggie wanted to please her coach and her parents, but she still went with her gut

91

feeling and sought treatment for her back pain. And it's a good thing because if Maggie would have practiced through the pain, she may have put herself at risk for a permanent injury, possibly ending her gymnastics career.

INTRODUCTION TO INJURIES TO THE LOWER BACK AND THORAX

Unfortunately, injuries to the lower back and thorax are common. In fact, in the United States, up to 80 percent of the general population will have some sort of episode of back pain at some point in their lives; some of these injuries will be the result of sports competition, and others will result from everyday activities.

The lower back and thorax comprised many layers of ligaments and muscles. The back muscles are among the strongest in the body, but many teen athletes still tend to ask too much of them. Almost all sports-related injuries to the lower back are affected by weak muscles. Back injuries can also result from tense muscles or strain during lifting. If back muscles are overloaded, the muscle fibers can pull or tear, causing spasms and pain. This pain can come from injured muscles, ligaments, joints, nerves, or in rare cases, organs.

Virtually any sport can result in a back injury, though back injuries tend to be more common in running, tennis, basketball, football, baseball, volleyball, and downhill skiing.

Because so many back injuries are caused by overloading the muscles, teenage athletes can help to prevent them by performing exercises that strengthen the lower back and abdominal/core muscles. The treatment regimen for most back injuries is essentially the same: When pain sets in, ice the area on and off for 20 to 30 minutes at a time, two to three times a day. In some cases, bed rest may help; but more than a day or two of bed rest can actually further weaken the muscles, so you should get up and try to move as soon as possible. Most back injuries also respond well to daily stretching and strengthening exercises. Once the acute stages of the injury are over, you can use heat to loosen your back before sports or other activity. Surgery is usually considered only as a last resort and is reserved for only a select few types of back injuries.

No matter what your diagnosis, if you have a back injury, you should be on the lookout for signs and symptoms of a serious injury to the spine. These include:

➤ Loss of bladder or bowel control
➤ Severe, constant pain

- Weakness in your legs
- Numbness or tingling in the pubic/groin region
- Fever
- Pain that awakens you at night

If you experience any of the above symptoms, seek emergency medical care immediately.

LUMBAR SPRAIN OR STRAIN

Lumbar sprains and strains can result from almost any sport, from contact sports such as football and rugby to recreational sports such as bowling. In fact, sprains and strains are the most common cause of lower and mid-back pain in athletes.

The symptoms of strains and sprains are very similar, and the treatments for both injuries are almost the same. Symptoms of a lumbar sprain or strain usually set in while an athlete is playing his or her sport and get worse over the 24 hours following. The pain, which comes from the overstretched ligaments or muscles, may be the worst about a day after the injury occurs.

Specific symptoms include the following:

- Pain in the lower back
- Stiffness in the lower back
- Spasm in the lower back
- Radiating pain into the buttocks
- Tenderness in the small area of the lower back
- Pain that gets worse with bending or arching the back
- Pain that improves while sitting or lying down

Initial self-treatment for a lumbar sprain or strain should include resting your back and applying ice to the painful area a few times a day. You should apply the ice for five-minute increments (five minutes on, five minutes off) for about 30 to 60 minutes. You can also try taking over-the-counter pain relievers such as ibuprofen (Advil) or acetaminophen (Tylenol). You should also avoid any activity that makes the pain worse.

If your symptoms worsen or don't improve in 48 hours, you should see your doctor. If you have a numb sensation in your buttocks, weakness in your lower limbs, or loss of bowel or bladder control, go to the emergency room immediately.

To diagnose a lumbar sprain or strain, your doctor will perform a physical examination to rule out more serious injuries. In general,

X-rays cannot show a lumbar strain or sprain, but they may be used to rule out different problems.

Once your doctor has determined that you indeed have a lumbar sprain or strain, he or she may prescribe one or more of the following treatments:

➤ More potent prescription anti-inflammatory medication
➤ Prescription muscle relaxants
➤ Physical therapy or osteopathic manipulation
➤ Chiropractic treatment
➤ Acupuncture

Physical therapy for lumbar sprains and strains will focus on stretching and strengthening exercises for the leg, exercises for the core/abdominal and lower back muscles to improve flexibility, and exercises that stabilize the spine and help to prevent future injury to the back.

In addition, your doctor may instruct you to continue to ice the area, or he or she may prescribe ultrasound or electrical stimulation to help ease pain and inflammation.

Once the pain of a lumbar sprain or strain has subsided and you can perform simple activities of daily life without stiffness, your doctor may give you the green light to return to your sport. If you feel any pain, you should stop the activity that is causing it, however. In most cases, athletes can return to play about three to six weeks after the injury occurred.

THORAX SPRAIN OR STRAIN

Thorax sprains and strains are similar to lumbar sprains and strains, except they occur higher up on the spine. Symptoms may develop slowly or come on suddenly in the middle of the back. They include:

➤ Muscle spasms
➤ Pain that radiates to different areas of the body
➤ Stiffness
➤ Headaches
➤ Digestive problems
➤ Rib pain
➤ Limited range of motion in the mid back

If you suspect a thorax sprain or strain, see your doctor. He or she may initially instruct you to rest your back and take over-the-counter pain relievers such as ibuprofen (Advil), acetaminophen (Tylenol), or naproxen sodium (Aleve). In addition, stretches and exercise are extremely important. Massage therapy is often a part of the treatment regimen.

SCHEUERMANN'S DISEASE

Scheuermann's disease, also called Scheuermann's kyphosis, is a condition that occurs when the upper part of the spine doesn't grow as fast as the back part of the spine. As a result, the vertebrae become wedge-shaped, with the narrow part of the wedge in front. This creates a curvature of the spine that gives the sufferer a "hunchback" appearance. Scheuermann's disease is more common in males, and it usually sets in toward the end of the growth spurt in adolescence. Most teens with Scheuermann's disease also have a mild case of scoliosis.

To diagnose Scheuermann's disease, your doctor will perform a physical exam and order an X-ray.

Treatment of Scheuermann's disease will depend on the severity of the condition. The goals of treatment are to ease pain, correct an unacceptable deformity, and prevent the curve from getting worse. In teens with Scheuermann's disease who have more than a year of growth left, the curvature may be partially reversed with use of a brace, called a Milwaukee brace. In addition, an exercise program that involves strengthening and stretching the back and legs may help alleviate pain.

Scheuermann's disease usually causes very few problems, if any, so physical therapy and home exercises are often all that is needed to allow normal participation in sports. Surgery is rarely required for Scheuermann's disease, but it may be necessary in severe cases in which the curve is greater than 70 degrees. The main goal of surgery is usually to correct the curvature, but it can also help to lessen pain.

BACK SPASM

A back muscle spasm can be so painful that an athlete is certain something else is wrong. You may be suddenly disabled by excruciating pain. In addition to pain, symptoms of a back spasm include a feeling of tension in the back, and in severe cases, a back that is tilted to one side as a result of the spasm and shortening muscle fibers.

If you are experiencing back pain and suspect a spasm, it's a good idea to rest for a few days. You may also try over-the-counter anti-inflammatory medication such as aspirin or naproxen sodium (Aleve) and ice the area on and off for 20 to 30 minutes at a time, two or three times a day. If the pain persists for more than a few days, see your doctor. He or she may prescribe other medications to relax the muscles and relieve the pain, as well as physical therapy. Supportive girdles are occasionally prescribed for the short term, but most doctors and therapists try to avoid using them because they can lead to muscle weakness, especially over time.

In most cases, physical therapy for a back spasm involves ice, then heat, electrical stimulation of the muscles, and deep massage to relax the muscles. This is usually followed by exercises to strengthen the back and help prevent future spasms.

DISC INJURIES

Discs are fibrous pillows that act as shock absorbers for the spine. Discs comprise an outer layer, which is fibrous and firm, called the annulus fibrosis, and an inner gelatinous layer, called the nucleus pulposis. Discs are found between the vertebrae, where they act as a cushion.

Sports that involve twisting and bending, such as golf, tennis, football (particularly the quarterback position), and baseball (particularly the pitcher position), put athletes at risk for disc injuries.

Disc injuries range from bulging discs to herniated discs to ruptured discs. Each of these injuries can cause pain in the back and/or legs, and possibly weakness, numbness, and tingling in the legs. The pain may get worse while straining (for example, when lifting heavy weights).

To diagnose a disc problem, your doctor will usually ask you a lot of questions, perform a physical exam, and may order an MRI. If a disc problem is confirmed, he or she will most likely start to treat the injury with rest and pain relievers and occasionally will prescribe steroids to reduce the inflammation. Beyond that, a physical therapy program that involves exercises to stretch and strengthen the area will help. Surgery is reserved as a last resort for a select few severe cases.

If at any point during the course of your treatment, you experience loss of bowel or bladder function, seek medical attention immediately. You may need emergency surgery.

Most athletes are allowed to return to their sport once they feel ready, usually after about four to six weeks of treatment. Heavy weight lifting usually needs to be avoided, at least until all pain is gone and muscles are strong, because it increases pressure within the disc.

SPONDYLOLYSIS (CRACKED BACK) AND SPONDYLOLISTHESIS

Spondylolysis is a stress fracture of the part of the vertebrae that connect the front and rear portions of the bone. The most common cause of low back pain in teen athletes that can be seen on an X-ray, spondylolysis often occurs in high-level athletes, especially gymnasts. It is typically the result of repeated hyperextension (bending backward) of the spine. Other sports that can cause the condition include weight lifting, swimming (especially the butterfly stroke), volleyball, and football (especially defensive linemen, who are holding the back in extension). Spondylolysis is more common in females than in males.

Spondylolysis may be present without symptoms, but when symptoms do occur, they include chronic back pain described as a dull lower backache that worsens while bending backward and occasionally radiates to the buttocks, or pain that spreads across the lower back and feels like a muscle strain. Hamstring tightness is very common; in fact, it is often the only symptom reported by the athlete.

If you are suffering from back pain that worsens during sports play or your everyday activities, see your doctor. He or she will perform a physical exam and may order an X-ray to take a closer look at your back. Even if the X-ray is normal, the doctor may further investigate with a test called a SPECT scan, which can also tell whether the fracture is old or new.

Regardless of whether the congenital fracture is old or new, your doctor will most likely tell you to reduce your activity level and prescribe exercises to strengthen your back until the symptoms go away. He or she may also instruct you to take over-the-counter pain medications or prescribe pain medication or muscle relaxants.

If your doctor discovers that the fracture just happened, he or she will instruct you to stop all physical activity and may prescribe a brace in an attempt to allow the fracture to heal. Your doctor may also tell you to take anti-inflammatory medications such as ibuprofen (Advil) to help reduce the pain.

In most cases, rest from aggravating activities followed by strengthening and flexibility exercises (including hamstring stretches) is all that is needed to return to athletic activity. Back braces are occasionally used, but long-term use is often discouraged because they can lead to further weakness in the back.

In cases where spondylolysis occurs bilaterally (on both sides), it may allow the vertebra to slip out of place, a condition called spondylolisthesis. This slippage is usually worsened by back extension and flexion, essentially the same activities that aggravate spondylolysis. The slippage may be mild or severe, and it may be stable or unstable. Mild cases are similar to spondylolysis and are treated similarly. Severe cases may lead to more serious problems, including pain, weakness, or numbness in the legs, though this is rather uncommon.

To diagnose spondylolisthesis, your doctor will perform a physical examination and order an X-ray. Your doctor will most likely order both flexion and extension X-rays to assess stability and the degree of the bone slippage. He or she will then grade the spondylolisthesis from I to V. Each progressive number represents a more severe slippage of the upper vertebra onto the one just below it. Grades I and II usually respond to nonsurgical treatments, but surgery is considered in athletes with grades III through V, or those with more severe or persistent symptoms (especially if they experience pain that radiates into the legs).

Physical therapy is an important part of recovery from both spondylolysis and spondylolisthesis and will most likely include both aerobic activity and stretching and strengthening exercises. Regaining flexibility in the hamstrings is crucial in allowing full return to athletic activity and preventing further injury. It is important that you stick to your physical therapy routine in order to minimize your chances of reinjury.

If you are recovering from spondylolysis or spondylolisthesis, you will not be allowed to participate in sports. You may be able to perform light low-impact exercise such as bicycling with the aid of the brace (if you were prescribed one). After you've adequately rested the area and regained appropriate strength and flexibility in your back and legs, you should be able to return to play. However, in certain cases of spondylolisthesis where the vertebra has slipped excessively, you may have to give up certain sports or activities that force you to arch your back violently, such as diving and gymnastics, or sports that put you at risk for a heavy blow to the back, such as basketball or football. In severe cases, where the slipped vertebra worsens despite treatment, surgery may be required.

In most cases, return to play after a diagnosis of acute spondylolysis or spondylolisthesis ranges from three to 12 months, depending on the severity of the injury and how quickly it heals. Return to play will be restricted to activities that do not cause pain.

COMPRESSION FRACTURE

A *compression fracture* is a fracture of a vertebra in the back of the spine. Compression fractures typically result from sports that cause a sudden flexing (bending forward) of the spine, such as football, gymnastics, track and field, and skiing. The spine flexes forward with such force that the vertebra actually collapses on itself.

Symptoms of a compression fracture include constant and severe pain that gets worse with any motion, but especially when the back is extended (bent backward).

If you experience the above symptoms, see your doctor. To diagnose a compression fracture, your doctor will order an X-ray. If the fracture is confirmed, treatment will depend on the severity of the fracture and ranges from pain medications and a brace for milder cases to surgery in more extreme cases.

Physical therapy and rehabilitation following a compression fracture focus on helping you regain the full motion in your back without pain. If you play a noncontact sport, you will probably be able to return to play in about 12 weeks if you have regained full range of motion and no longer have pain. If you play a contact sport such as football, you will have to weigh the pros and cons of returning to play as further injury to your back could cause permanent pain. Discuss the risk-to-benefit ratio of returning to your sport with your doctor.

BURST FRACTURE

A *burst fracture* is caused by a simultaneous flexion and loading of the spine; for example, when a football player becomes airborne during a tackle and lands hard on the ground. The force of the trauma causes the vertebrae to literally burst apart and shatter. Because the bone is shattered, pieces of it can become lodged in the spinal canal. In the most severe case, a piece of the vertebra actually injures the spinal cord. In addition to football players, gymnasts, rock climbers, and horseback riders are at risk for burst fractures.

Burst fractures are medical emergencies, and, therefore, they should be treated with extreme caution. If you or a fellow player suffers a trauma on the field and experiences severe spine pain, with or without weakness in the arms and legs, do not move. Wait until a trained professional can transfer you from the field to the emergency room. If a burst fracture propels a piece of bone into the spinal cord, the injury could result in paralysis.

Initial management in the emergency room usually involves intravenous steroids and an MRI, and then there's a good chance surgery will be necessary. This is all usually followed by rehabilitation, often in a rehabilitative center. Recovery may take several months or more, and return to high-risk sports is often not allowed.

PREVENTING BACK INJURIES

Since weakness of the back muscles contributes to most back injuries, the best way to prevent these injuries is to strengthen your back.

Back strengthening programs should focus on strengthening both the flexor and extensor muscles in the back, as well as the abdominal muscles. Strong, flexible muscles around the abdomen and lower back will help to stabilize the spine and prevent injury. The flexor muscles pull your back forward and down, and the extensor muscles help to lift your back into an erect position.

If you suffer from chronic back pain, you may have to avoid sports and activities that stress and strain your back. Sports that can cause and aggravate back problems include running, tennis, aerobics, golf, basketball, volleyball, downhill skiing, bowling, football, dancing, baseball, and any other sport that involves back twisting or arching or sudden stops and starts.

Perhaps even more important than preventing sports-related back injuries is learning how to perform everyday activities without straining your back. To prevent back strain, do the following:

- Maintain consistent good posture with your shoulders back.
- Support your lower back with a pillow while sitting.
- When lifting a heavy object from the floor, squat as close as possible to the object and lift with your legs instead of your back. Remember: The muscles in the front of your thighs are some of the strongest muscles on your body.
- When you lift, lift smoothly; fast lifts put more stress on your spine.
- Don't bend at the waist when lifting.
- Before you lift an object, get a sense of how heavy it is.
- Avoid carrying heavy luggage or briefcases; use a luggage roller whenever possible.
- Whenever you are doing prolonged back-straining activities such as gardening, scrubbing a floor, etc., kneel on one knee instead of bending at the waist.
- Don't wear high heels; wear flats instead.

EXERCISES THAT IMPROVE BACK STRENGTH AND FLEXIBILITY

Toe touch. Standing with your feet shoulder-width apart, bend forward at the waist and lower your forehead between your knees while you stand. Go down as far as you can go, then grasp behind

Spondylolisthesis: Why Is It So Common in Teens?

Spondylolisthesis is a condition in which one of the vertebrae of the spine slips out of place onto the vertebra below it. If the vertebra slips too far, it can press on a nerve, causing pain, though this is relatively uncommon.

Spondylolisthesis is a common cause of lower back pain in teenagers. Symptoms, including back pain that spreads across the lower back and feels like a muscle strain, as well as tightness in hamstrings, usually begin during the teenage growth spurt. (In some cases of spondylolisthesis, symptoms occur earlier, however.)

Spondylolisthesis is so common in teenagers because teenagers frequently engage in sports that put them at risk for the condition, such as weight lifting and gymnastics. This, coupled with the fast growth spurt most adolescents experience in their teen years, puts them at risk for the condition.

Luckily, in most cases, surgery is not required to treat spondylolisthesis. The condition usually responds well to rest, over-the-counter pain medication, and strengthening/flexibility exercises.

your knees and try to go a little farther. Hold that position for 10 to 15 seconds. Start with three repetitions and increase by one every other day until you reach 12 repetitions.

Toe touch with rotation. Stand with your legs spread. Bend forward at the waist and drop your head down so that your forehead is over your knee. Hold for 10 to 15 seconds. Then stand up straight again and repeat on your left side. Start with three repetitions and increase gradually by one every other day until you reach 12 repetitions.

Knee pull with head curl. Lie on your back with your knees bent and your feet flat on the floor. Bring one knee up toward your chest and clasp it with both hands. Pull your knee down gently toward your chest and curl your head up slightly at the same time. Hold for 10 to 15 seconds. Then repeat with the other leg. Start with three repetitions and increase gradually by one every other day until you reach 12 repetitions.

Pelvic tilt. Lie on your back with your knees bent and your feet flat on the floor. Relax your back muscles and tighten your abdominal and buttocks muscles in order to press your back flat against the floor until your back is completely flat. Start with three repetitions and increase gradually by one every other day until you reach 12 repetitions.

Back extension. Stand up straight with your feet shoulder-width apart and your arms straight at your sides. Slowly lean your upper body backward from your waist and try to look at the ceiling. Hold for 10 seconds, then relax and straighten up. Do five repetitions and build up by two repetitions as the stretch becomes easier.

Abdominal curl. Lie on your back with your knees bent and your feet flat on the floor. Clasp your hands behind your head and slowly curl your shoulder blades up off the floor, leaving your back on the floor. Hold for five seconds and then slowly lower your head and shoulders back to the floor. Start with five repetitions and increase the number by five as the exercise gets easier.

Hurdler stretch. While standing, put one foot on a chair in front of you so that your leg is straight and parallel to the ground. Then bend your forehead forward and try to touch it to your knee. Hold for 10 to 15 seconds. Then repeat with the other leg. Start with three repetitions and increase gradually by one every other day until you reach 12 repetitions.

WHAT YOU NEED TO KNOW

➤ Because so many back injuries are caused by overloading the muscles, teenage athletes can help to prevent them by performing exercises that strengthen the lower back and abdominal muscles.

➤ No matter what your diagnosis, if you have a back injury, you should be on the lookout for signs and symptoms of a serious injury to the spine. These include:
  • Loss of bladder or bowel control
  • Severe, constant pain
  • Weakness in your legs

If you experience any of the above symptoms, seek emergency medical care immediately.

> ▶ If you suffer from chronic back pain, you may have to avoid sports and activities that stress and strain your back. Sports that can cause and aggravate back problems include running, tennis, aerobics, golf, basketball, volleyball, downhill skiing, bowling, football, dancing, baseball, and any other sport that involves back twisting or arching or sudden stops and starts. Sports that may put less strain on your back include swimming (certain strokes), walking, cross-country skiing, bicycling (if your back is in a comfortable position), and stationary bicycling.

8

Hip Injuries

Jane, 16, has been running cross-country since she was in middle school. Now that she's a junior, she has become more focused, with the goal of being the top female runner on the team in her senior year. To do this, Jane has logged a tremendous amount of mileage lately. At the same time, she's also begun to eat less, fearing that junk food will hinder her performance. As a result, Jane has lost 10 pounds quickly, and her periods have stopped. She's also begun to notice a nagging pain in her groin area that gets worse as she runs.

Jane is showing the classic signs of something called "the female athlete triad," which consists of poor nutrition, amenorrhea (the absence of periods), and osteoporosis. The weakening of Jane's bones as a result of her malnutrition has most likely led to a stress fracture in her hip, a common injury in teenagers with the female athlete triad. Jane needs to see her doctor for a diagnosis for her hip pain. When he or she talks with Jane, her doctor will probably suspect the female athlete triad and refer Jane for psychological counseling in addition to rehabilitation for her injury.

A stress fracture is one of many injuries that teenage athletes can suffer in their hips. This chapter will cover some of the most common injuries of the hips, as well as what teen athletes can do to help prevent and treat them.

INTRODUCTION TO HIP INJURIES

The hip is a ball-and-socket joint in which the ball fits very snugly into the socket. This tight fit makes the joint stable, in contrast with more shallow joints like the shoulder. However, as a key weight-bearing joint, hip injuries do occur in teenage athletes, particularly for those playing basketball, football, rugby, hockey, lacrosse, running, track and field, golf, and volleyball. When hip injuries do occur, they should not be ignored. Here are some of the most common:

ADDUCTOR STRAIN (GROIN PULL)

The *adductor muscles* are the muscles of the inner thigh. An adductor strain, or groin pull, usually occurs all of a sudden, when an athlete quickly contracts these muscles, such as during cutting maneuvers while rapidly changing direction from side to side. Hockey and soccer players are most at risk for adductor strains, but teen athletes who play any sport can suffer this injury, particularly athletes who have less experience or who are just starting a season. Other risk factors for a groin pull include a previous adductor strain and poor flexibility or strength in the hip joint.

You can suspect an adductor strain if you experience sudden pain in the middle of your thigh or groin after twisting your leg a certain way during sports play. See your doctor for a diagnosis; he or she will perform a physical exam and may order an X-ray and/or MRI to make sure nothing else is wrong.

Initially, treatment for an adductor strain involves RICE and crutches, if you need them. Groin straps, typically made of neoprene, are occasionally used to support the tendons during activity but are difficult to properly position and may be uncomfortable. When the pain subsides, you will be able to start exercises to help strengthen and stretch your adductor muscles. Stretching is particularly important to help prevent reinjury to the area. Steroid injections are occasionally considered for persistent cases. Surgery is rarely necessary and is reserved for acute tendon ruptures or chronic pain that has not responded to conservative treatment.

You will be able to return to play once you have regained the flexibility and strength in your groin and can easily play your sport without pain. In most cases, this takes about one to six weeks, but often takes much longer.

ADDUCTOR TENDONITIS

Adductor tendonitis—or tendonitis of the adductor muscles in the inner thigh—is basically a more chronic version of the adductor strain described above, and it is rather common in teenage athletes. Over time, the strain put on the legs and hips by sports such as hockey, gymnastics, horseback riding, running, and kickboxing can cause tiny tears (called microtears) in the muscles of the hip adductors. Adductor tendonitis usually develops slowly over time, gradually progressing from an annoyance to an injury that keeps an athlete immobilized. At its worst, adductor tendonitis causes pain almost all the time, even at rest.

Symptoms of adductor tendonitis include pain in the upper thigh and groin. To diagnose adductor tendonitis, your doctor will perform a physical examination and perhaps order an ultrasound or MRI to pinpoint the exact location of the injury.

Treatment for adductor tendonitis typically includes physical therapy, over-the-counter or prescription pain relievers or anti-inflammatory medications, and occasionally a steroid injection. Physical therapy includes stretching, therapeutic massage, exercises to strengthen the muscles of the hip, and transcutaneous electrical nerve stimulation (TENS). Unfortunately, physical therapy only works for about a third of people with adductor tendonitis. If these more conservative treatments aren't effective within six months, surgery may be considered.

You will be able to return to play following adductor tendonitis as soon as the pain has subsided, which may take several months. In some cases, athletes never regain the full level of ability they had before the injury.

SPORTS HERNIA

A *sports hernia* is a tear in the muscles of the lower abdomen that can cause the muscle to pull away from the bones of the hip. Sports hernias are caused by a weakness in the muscles of the abdominal wall. Sports that involve cutting, twisting, jumping, or pulling motions repeatedly stress some of the tissues in the lower abdomen and can lead to a sports hernia.

Symptoms of a sports hernia include gradually worsening pain in the lower abdomen or groin. In males, it may be present in a testicle. While other forms of abdominal hernias involve a visible mass, this isn't usually the case with sports hernia.

Diagnosis of a sports hernia is often quite difficult since there is no accurate test for the condition. Patients who have a sports hernia typically have persisting groin pain with cutting movements yet have negative results on all diagnostic tests, which are mostly helpful to make sure you don't have a different type of injury. The best way to diagnose a sports hernia is through a detailed description of which specific activities are causing pain, followed by a careful physical examination.

Treatment for a sports hernia begins with RICE, and in some cases, physical therapy. If these conservative treatments don't work, or if the case is persistent and severe, surgery is then considered. There are very few physicians who specialize in this surgery, which is usually done by a general surgeon, not an orthopedic surgeon.

Return to play after a sports hernia varies widely—from six weeks to six months—depending on the extent of the injury and whether or not it was treated surgically.

OSTEITIS PUBIS

Osteitis pubis is inflammation of the area where the right and left pubic bones meet in the front of the pelvis. The condition is often seen in athletes who play contact sports such as football, rugby, and hockey, as well as some noncontact sports such as running, soccer, and basketball. Over time, the repetitive stress of one leg swinging in these activities puts strain on the tendons in this area.

Symptoms of osteitis pubis include pain in the middle of the pelvis that may or may not be accompanied by slight swelling or bruising. The pain usually comes on suddenly and gets worse when the athlete tries to jog, walk briskly, or run. If the condition goes untreated, the pain may spread to the groin region and the inner thighs.

To diagnose osteitis, a doctor will perform a physical examination and possibly an X-ray or MRI.

If the condition is confirmed, for the first two weeks treatment will involve resting the area, specifically from any activities that involve sprinting, forceful side-to-side kicking, and jumping. Anti-inflammatory medication, ice, and/or heat may also be used at this time. If pain still persists after the first 14 days, physical therapy is the next step. Physical therapy will most likely include exercises to improve strength and flexibility in the hip, ultrasound, and manual treatment/therapeutic massage. Once pain subsides, you will be able to begin reconditioning by jogging, walking, or using a stationary bike. In rare cases, surgery is required.

In order to return to play following osteitis, you must be completely pain-free and able to perform all aspects of your sport comfortably. The amount of time it takes athletes to return to play following osteitis varies, depending on the severity of the injury.

HIP POINTER

A *hip pointer*, characterized by pain directly on the hip bone, is usually caused by a blow to the hip. This blow can come from an object such as a football helmet, lacrosse stick, or baseball. Or an athlete may suffer a hip pointer after being tackled on frozen turf or sliding too forcefully into home plate.

The classic symptom of a hip pointer is pain along the top of the hip bone where it is at its boniest. Hip pointers can also occur on other areas of the hip where there are boney protrusions. Pain with a hip pointer gets worse when you try to do a sit-up or attempt to swing your leg sideways away from your body. Swelling or bruising over the painful area could indicate a more serious injury, such as a fracture.

To diagnose a hip pointer, your doctor will perform a physical examination and may order an X-ray and/or MRI. Initial treatment will include icing the area five minutes on, five minutes off, for 30 to 40 minutes, four times per day for the first 72 hours, and wrapping the area with a compression wrap in between icings. After the first 72 hours, if you do not have extensive bruising or intolerable pain, you will be instructed to perform gentle stretching exercises. Treatment may also include ultrasound to provide deep heat to the tissues, as well as electrical stimulation. If walking is painful, you may also need crutches to provide temporary immobilization.

Return to play following a hip pointer will depend on the severity of the injury. In the case of a simple hip pointer, you may be able to return to play in a week or so. If it is more severe and involves small tears in the surrounding muscles, it may take two to four weeks for you to be able to return to play without pain and stiffness. In the case of a more severe hip pointer, your doctor may prescribe a compression-resistant pad to protect your hip bone once you get back in the game. You may also be able to return to play earlier with injections of an anesthetic agent on game day. This is usually not recommended for high school athletes, however.

HIP FLEXOR STRAIN

Your hip flexor muscles allow you to lift your knee and bend at the waist. These muscles can become strained with overuse when you repeatedly flex your knee or perform high kicks. Therefore, hip flexor strains are most common in soccer players, bicyclists, track and field athletes, and teenagers who practice martial arts.

Symptoms of a hip flexor strain include pain in the groin area, mostly in front where your thigh meets your pelvis. You may notice pain when you try to lift your thigh at the hip, either while lying, sitting, or walking/running. There may also be a snapping sensation.

Two commonly injured hip flexors include the iliopsoas and the sartorius muscles. They are often injured in teenage athletes who perform repetitive hip flexion motions, such as runners, gymnasts, soccer players, and dancers.

To diagnose a hip flexor strain, your doctor will perform a physical examination to look for tenderness in the area of your hip flexors.

Treatment for a hip flexor strain may include icing the area on and off for 20 to 30 minutes every three to four hours for two to three days, or until the pain subsides. In addition, your doctor may prescribe anti-inflammatory medications or instruct you to purchase them over the counter. Treatment will also include exercises to strengthen and stretch your hip flexor muscles. As you are recovering, you may be advised to perform some sort of cross training, such as swimming.

Return to play following a hip flexor strain depends on the severity of the injury and the athlete's individual response to treatment. In general, the longer you wait to seek treatment for a hip flexor strain, the longer it will take you to heal. You will be able to return to play safely when you can run straight ahead with a normal stride and without pain, have full range of motion in your leg, and are able to jump on both legs at the same time and the injured leg by itself without pain.

GREATER TROCHANTERIC BURSITIS AND GLUTEUS MEDIUS TENDONITIS

Greater trochanteric bursitis (bursitis of the hip), which involves inflammation of one or more of the bursae in the hip, is a common injury in teen athletes. The hip abductor tendons are commonly affected, including the gluteus medius and the *iliotibial band* (ITB). Sports that cause the hip to rotate repeatedly, such as long-distance running, put athletes at particular risk.

Symptoms of bursitis of the hip include pain on the outside of the thigh that radiates down to the outside of the knee. Pain commonly strikes at night when the athlete is trying to get comfortable in bed. Activities that make symptoms worse include walking, running, and climbing.

To diagnose bursitis of the hip, your doctor will take your history and perform a physical examination. He or she may also measure your legs to make sure the injury isn't due to a leg-length discrepancy. MRI or ultrasound are usually not necessary but may be done in severe or persistent cases.

Treatment for bursitis of the hip includes rest, ice and/or heat, strengthening and flexibility exercises, therapeutic ultrasound, over-the-counter or prescription pain relievers, anti-inflammatory medications, and occasionally, corticosteroid injections. If the injury is mild, anti-inflammatory medications and rest alone may do the trick.

You may return to play following bursitis of the hip when the pain subsides, which usually takes a few weeks. When you do return to play, you should ease back into your sport and rest as soon as you feel any pain.

SNAPPING HIP SYNDROME

Snapping hip syndrome is caused by many different problems. It often results when the tendons of the hip "snap" over bone protuberances. Common areas for this to occur are the iliopsoas tendon and the ilio-tibial band (both mentioned above). Snapping hip might also be due to tears in the hip cartilage called the labrum. Runners, cheerleaders, and dancers are particularly prone to snapping hip syndrome. The motions in these sports cause the tendon to "snap" over the hip like a bow.

The most prominent symptom of snapping hip syndrome is a snapping sensation in the hip. Other symptoms may include pain while bearing weight on the affected leg, a feeling of instability in the hip, and restricted range of motion.

To diagnose snapping hip syndrome, your doctor will perform a physical exam and attempt to catch the snapping sensation. To treat the injury, your doctor will prescribe exercises to help stretch and strengthen your hip. He or she may also tell you to avoid activities that cause the snapping and to take over-the-counter anti-inflammatory medications to help ease the pain. If symptoms persist, you may need a cortisone shot or surgery.

If your injury doesn't require surgery and you are diligent about doing the exercises prescribed for you, you will probably be able to return to your sport in two to three weeks following a diagnosis of snapping hip syndrome.

STRESS FRACTURE OF THE HIP/PELVIS

In the case of a stress fracture, hip pain—which exists on the back of the thigh—develops gradually. The pain usually worsens when the athlete hops on the affected leg.

Pelvic stress fractures usually occur in a group of four bones called the pubic rami, in the front of the pelvis, but they can also occur at the top of the femur bone. They are most common in long-distance runners because the repetitive pounding transfers a force from the legs to the pelvis. Teenagers and amenorrheic women (women who do not get a period) are most vulnerable to pelvic stress fractures.

Symptoms of a pelvic stress fracture include pain in the pelvis or groin area that gets worse with activity. If you are experiencing these symptoms, particularly if you are a long-distance runner, see your doctor. He or she will order an X-ray, bone scan, or MRI to look for a fracture.

If a stress fracture is confirmed, the treatment will include RICE (often nonweight-bearing), over-the-counter or prescription pain medication or anti-inflammatory medication, and addressing the cause of the injury. Potential causes include nutritional deficiencies, hormonal imbalances, biomechanical imbalances (anywhere from back/pelvis to the feet), and overtraining. If you are a female, your doctor may also screen you for a syndrome called the female athlete triad, which includes amenorrhea (absence of a menstrual period), osteoporosis, and a poor diet or eating disorder. If signs point to the female athlete triad, you may also be referred for counseling.

Depending on the severity and cause of a hip or pelvic stress fracture, you may be able to return to activity in about four to six weeks. You should advance slowly and only under the close supervision of a physician, and you should modify any part of your training regimen that could have contributed to the injury in the first place. For instance, if you are a runner, you will need to start your mileage at approximately 20 percent of your preinjury level and gradually increase it over several months (typically no more than 10 percent per week). Before you return, you should build up strength and flexibility in your hip with exercises prescribed by your doctor or physical therapist. If you are a runner, a thorough evaluation of your running shoes by an expert is essential. This should include a gait analysis in various shoes to make sure the shoe is allowing the best foot mechanics. Occasionally, either store bought athletic inserts or custom-made orthotics will be recommended.

PELVIC AVULSION FRACTURES

More common in teenagers than adults, pelvic avulsion fractures can occur in a few different places in the hip area, depending on the sport played. Jumping sports such as basketball and volleyball tend to lead to pelvic avulsion fractures on the hip bone itself. Kicking sports such as soccer and football can cause this type of fracture in the front part of the hip. Running sports can lead to a pelvic avulsion fracture in the bone you sit on, called the ischial tuberosity.

Symptoms of a pelvic avulsion fracture include pain that comes on suddenly in a specific area of the hip (usually one of the three areas mentioned above). This pain may or may not be associated with a snapping or popping sound. The pain may get worse when you touch the area or try to move your hip.

Treatment for a pelvic avulsion fracture will depend where on the hip it occurs. If the fracture takes place on the front of the hip, treatment will include rest, ice, and pain medication until the fracture heals. If the avulsion fractures occur on the hip bone or the bone you sit on, surgery may be necessary, depending on the severity of the injury.

You will be able to return to play following a pelvic avulsion fracture when there is callus formation in the fracture (your doctor will test for this) and you have recovered full strength and flexibility. This can take anywhere from six weeks to four months.

HIP LABRAL TEAR

The labrum is a piece of cartilage that attaches to the hip joint and helps provide hip stability. There are a number of nerve endings in the labrum, which is why this injury can be particularly painful. Labral tears can be acute, resulting from a football tackle or a skiing mishap, or they can result from the repetitive stress of running, skating, or golf. Depending on the nature of the injury, the tear can occur anywhere on the labrum.

Symptoms of a hip labral tear include pain anywhere on the hip, from the front to the buttocks, depending on the location of the injury. The front part of the labrum is the most frequently injured section, and this tear leads to pain when kicking or thrusting the hip forward. Tears in the back part of the labrum cause pain when thrusting the hip backward. There may also be a snapping sensation in the hip.

To diagnose a labral tear, your doctor will perform a physical examination and take X-rays of the hip to look for other conditions. Since X-rays do not show a labral tear, an MRI may be ordered, occasionally with an arthrogram, during which a dye is injected into the hip before the MRI to help better see a tear.

If you are diagnosed with a hip labral tear, you should first avoid all activities that cause pain in your hip. In some cases, rest alone will heal the injury. If not, your doctor may order a cortisone shot, crutches, and/or rehabilitative exercises that restore strength and flexibility. In severe cases, surgery may be required.

You will be able to return to play when the strength and range of motion on your injured side equals that of your uninjured side. If surgery is required, return to play may take up to six months.

BROKEN HIP

A broken hip (or hip fracture) is a serious acute injury that causes severe pain and the inability to move your hip or walk. Although rare in teenage athletes, broken hips can occur; when they do, they are usually caused by contact sports such as football.

Symptoms of a broken hip include severe pain, an inability to move the hip or leg, and a leg that appears shortened. In addition, the foot on the affected side may be rolled to the outside while the other foot points up.

A broken hip is a medical emergency. If you suspect a broken hip, do not move. Wait for an emergency medical team to help you get up and move you off the field. Treatment for a broken hip usually requires surgery.

SLIPPED CAPITAL FEMORAL EPIPHYSIS (SCFE)

As children approach adolescence, the growing end of the femur (thigh bone) can slip from the ball of the hip joint, leading to a condition called *slipped capital femoral epiphysis* (SCFE). SCFE results in a limp and problems rotating the leg inward. This condition usually sets in around age 12 for girls and 13.5 for boys—right around the biggest growth spurt. It is slightly more common in boys, and it affects both legs in 20 to 40 percent of cases.

More than 90 percent of cases of SCFE are "stable," meaning the person with the condition can walk without crutches. The remaining 10 percent of "unstable" SCFE cases usually result from an acute trauma, such as a fall or a sports injury.

Congenital Hip Problems and Sports Performance

If you are a teenager who plays sports and you start to feel pain in your hip, chances are it's a sports-related injury. It is possible, however, that the nagging pain in your hip could be due to a congenital hip problem that's just emerging a little later than usual (most congenital hip problems are diagnosed in childhood).

Symptoms of stable SCFE include stiffness in the hip, which may improve with rest. After a while, however, this stiffness may progress to pain and a limp. The pain can be felt in the groin, thigh, or knee—it doesn't necessarily affect the hip itself. As the condition progresses, a teenager with SCFE may lose the ability to move the hip, and the affected leg may twist outward. Playing sports or performing simple tasks like bending over to tie shoes may become difficult or impossible.

Symptoms of unstable SCFE include extreme pain, similar to the pain of a broken bone, and an inability to move the affected leg.

To diagnose either stable or unstable SCFE, your doctor will perform a physical examination and take X-rays of your pelvis and thigh area. If SCFE is confirmed, your doctor will most likely refer you to a childhood orthopedic surgeon, as surgery is usually required.

If SCFE is caught early enough, there is a good chance that you will recover completely and eventually be able to return to your sport, especially if you have stable SCFE—this is why a prompt diagnosis is important. You will need to use crutches for four to six weeks after the surgery, but after that, with the approval of your doctor, you will be able to return to your normal activities.

CONGENITAL HIP DYSPLASIA

Congenital hip dysplasia is a malformation of the hip joint, where the ball at the top of the thighbone isn't stable in its socket. As a result, the ligaments of the hip joint become loose and stretched. The degree of instability of the hip joint varies from child to child, and it usually gets worse as the child gets older.

Congenital hip dysplasia is usually diagnosed at birth or shortly after. A doctor can diagnose the condition with a physical exam coupled with an X-ray. However, some people with congenital hip dysplasia are not diagnosed with the condition until they reach adolescence, when they start to experience pain in their hip and groin areas during sports play or everyday life.

Luckily, congenital hip dysplasia can still be treated in adolescence and young adulthood, although the surgical methods used are more involved. After surgery, special exercises can help strengthen the hip, increase range of motion, and control pain.

PERTHES DISEASE

Perthes disease (also called Legg-Calve-Perthes disease) is a condition that causes necrosis of the femoral head (ball) that fits into the socket in the hip joint. Necrosis means the blood supply to the femoral head is cut off, which causes some of the bone to die. The body breaks down this dead bone, which leads to deformity and weakness in the hip joint.

Symptoms of Perthes disease usually set in between age three and 12 and include the ability to flex and extend the hip but not rotate it. The condition also causes pain in the hip and in most cases a limp.

Treatment of Perthes disease depends on the age of the patient and the amount of the femoral head that's affected. The goal of treatment is to keep the softened part of the femoral head within its socket so the socket can act as a mold and help keep the head round. Although people with Perthes disease may never have hips that are completely normal, it is possible to decrease pain and improve range of motion to the point that all activities are possible.

Keeping the hip moving is also important. Like clay on a wheel, a joint needs full range of motion to form properly. Therefore, if Perthes disease is caught early enough, range-of-motion exercises can keep the femoral head from becoming deformed.

Braces that keep the hip positioned out to the side are also frequently used to treat Perthes disease. These braces keep the femoral head deeper in its socket, helping it to keep its round shape. They must be worn for at least two years to allow the hip to remodel.

In advanced cases of Perthes disease, where the femoral head is already deformed, surgery is the only option.

PREVENTING HIP INJURIES

In many cases, there isn't much that can be done to prevent hip injuries, especially hip injuries that happen suddenly or result from

What is a hip pointer?

A hip pointer is an acute, painful injury to an area of the pelvis called the iliac crest. This is a fancy term for your hip bone. Hip pointers usually result from a direct blow to the hip from a fall on a hard surface or a collision with a football helmet. As a result, the hip bone and the muscles that overlay it become bruised. This leads to intense pain that can be felt when walking, coughing, laughing, and in some cases, even breathing deeply.

congenital problems. Hip injuries that result from overuse, however, can be prevented.

Hip injuries involving muscles, tendons, and ligaments are best prevented by warming up properly before you engage in your sport. Exercises that strengthen and stretch the hip will also help (see below for hip strengthening and stretching exercises).

Sleeping on your back (not your stomach or side) on a good, supportive mattress will also help. You should also avoid sleeping with pillows under your lower back or beneath your knees. If you are a runner, make sure you've had your running shoes properly evaluated by an expert, preferably using a video gait analysis. Athletic inserts or custom orthotics should be used if necessary.

EXERCISES TO HELP STRETCH AND STRENGTHEN THE HIP

Side straddle stretch. Stand with your legs about three feet apart. Keeping your trunk straight, gradually bend the knee on your uninjured side, then lean to that side, away from your injured hip. Hold the stretch for 20 to 30 seconds.

Yoga lotus stretch. Sit down and bend your knees so that the soles of your feet touch each other. Put your elbows on your knees and gradually push your knees outward and down. Hold for 20 to 30 seconds.

WHAT YOU NEED TO KNOW

▶ In general, the longer you wait to seek treatment for a hip injury, the longer it will take to heal.

▶ A broken hip is a medical emergency. If you suspect a broken hip, do not move. Wait for an emergency medical team to help you get up and move off the field.

▶ In many cases, there isn't much that can be done to prevent hip injuries, especially hip injuries that happen suddenly or result from congenital problems. Hip injuries that result from overuse, however, can be prevented.

▶ Hip injuries that involve muscles, tendons, and ligaments are best prevented by warming up properly before you engage in your sport.

9

Knee and Leg Injuries

Caitlin, 17, has been playing field hockey since she was in middle school. During her last game, as she cut in to hit a shot on goal, Caitlin felt a sharp pain in her knee and heard a loud popping sound. She fell to the ground, clutching her knee in pain. As her school trainer bent down beside her, Caitlin heard her utter the dreaded phrase: "torn ACL." Her heart sank—would this get in the way of the field hockey scholarship she had just gotten to her dream college?

When she got to the emergency room, Caitlin's fears were confirmed—she had torn her anterior cruciate ligament (ACL). But she was encouraged when her doctor explained that the surgery for ACL tears has evolved considerably over the past several years. He assured her that the surgery to repair the ACL would best enable her to return to full participation in field hockey well before she was scheduled to start playing in college—very good news for Caitlin and for other teen athletes who suffer injuries to their ACLs.

An anterior cruciate ligament tear is one of many knee and lower leg injuries that teenage athletes suffer. This chapter will cover some of the most common injuries of the knee and lower leg, as well as what teen athletes can do to help prevent and treat them.

THE KNEE

The knee is a hinge joint between the femur (thigh) and the *tibia* (lower leg). A complex joint, the knee helps the leg bend, straighten, twist, and rotate. Because it is a weight-bearing joint subject to so many different motions, the knee relies heavily on the muscles, tendons, and ligaments that support it and the cartilage that cushions it. A variety of motions can stress or tear any of these tissues. As a result, knee injuries—both overuse and acute—are extremely common in teen athletes; in fact, the knee is the most frequently injured joint in the body.

Most knee pain is the result of acute or chronic injuries. However, it is also important to rule out conditions unrelated to sports activity, including infection, arthritis, malignancy, or problems coming from the hip.

PATELLOFEMORAL SYNDROME/ RUNNER'S KNEE

Patellofemoral syndrome—or pain at the front of the knee—is the most common overuse knee injury found in teenage athletes. The injury, also known as "runner's knee," results from misalignment of the kneecap in its groove. Normally, the kneecap slides up and down in its groove as the knee bends and straightens. But if the kneecap is misaligned, it will pull to one side and rub on the side of the groove. Over time, this may cause the cartilage on the back of the kneecap and the side of the groove to wear away.

The underlying cause of runner's knee is often not the knee—it may be the back, pelvis, or even the foot; almost any mechanical imbalance may cause the kneecap to track unevenly.

Symptoms of patellofemoral syndrome include pain at the front of the knee that gets worse during activities that require you to flex your knee, such as running or jumping. It is very common for the pain to be aggravated when you go down stairs or hills. The pain may also worsen while you're sitting or driving—this is called the "theater sign" of runner's knee because it makes it difficult to sit through an entire movie or play without getting up to stretch. In some cases, fluid builds up and causes swelling. Your knee may also buckle when you try to stand.

If you suspect runner's knee, see your doctor. To diagnose the injury, he or she will perform a physical examination of your knee and perhaps of your entire lower extremity, from the pelvis to the foot.

Treatment for runner's knee first involves physical therapy or a home exercise program to increase strength and flexibility. Most commonly, the goal is to stretch the hamstrings and iliotibial band (ITB) in the outer knee and to strengthen the quadriceps muscles. Your doctor may also prescribe anti-inflammatory medication to decrease pain and swelling. In some cases, ultrasound or electrical stimulation may help to speed healing, as may an adjustable knee brace called a patellofemoral brace. Your doctor may also prescribe athletic inserts or custom-made orthotics if you have biomechanical problems in your feet (i.e., overpronation) that could be contributing to the problem. If these more conservative treatment methods don't work after six months, your doctor may order an X-ray or MRI to rule out other causes of the pain. In rare extreme cases, surgery may be performed to correct the tracking problem in the knee. If your doctor recommends surgery to correct the tracking, it is a good idea to get a second opinion since surgery might actually worsen the problem.

Return to play following patellofemoral syndrome can take anywhere from days to months, depending on the severity of the injury and whether or not it required surgery. Patellofemoral braces are often very effective in helping patients return to activity sooner, but they do not replace the need for continued physical therapy or home exercises. In order to return to play, you should be able to perform all motions of your sport without pain; if any pain or weakness remain, more physical therapy will be necessary. To prevent runner's knee from recurring, you may need to change your running shoe or perhaps wear an orthotic to help with proper foot mechanics.

ILIOTIBIAL BAND SYNDROME

The *iliotibial band* (ITB) is part of a tough muscle on the outside of the thigh and knee that runs from the lower part of the quadriceps to the bottom of the knee joint. ITB syndrome—or irritation of the ITB—most commonly results from an increase in training volume in runners, cyclists, and triathletes, but it can occur in teen athletes who play other sports as well. In the case of cyclists, position on the bike may contribute to the injury. For runners, wearing the wrong type of shoe may be a factor.

The main symptom of ITB syndrome is pain on the outside of the knee. In many cases, the rest of the knee is pain-free. The pain usually gets worse with continued activity; for example, a runner will notice it after he or she is a few miles into a workout.

To diagnose ITB syndrome, your doctor will perform a physical exam and possibly order an X-ray to rule out other causes of the pain. Treatment will usually involve rest and physical therapy. Because it is difficult to adequately stretch the ITB on your own, it is best to have a physical therapist assist with stretching. Ultrasound and electrical stimulation on the outside of the knee may also be helpful. An ITB strap can also help by providing some support to the area during activities. Other possible treatments include anti-inflammatory medications, ice, and cortisone injections.

Athletes with ITB syndrome may return to play when they can perform daily activities such as stair climbing or pedaling on a stationary bike without pain, which may in some cases take more than six weeks.

To prevent reinjury of the ITB, cyclists should have their biking position evaluated, and runners should consult with a physical trainer to assess whether or not they are wearing the right shoes. In some cases, orthotics may help. Athletes who have suffered ITB syndrome should also continue to stretch the ITB.

PATELLAR TENDONITIS (JUMPER'S KNEE)

The patellar tendon connects the *patella* (kneecap) to the front of the *tibia* (shin bone) at a protrusion called the tibial tuberosity (the bump under the kneecap). The patellar tendon acts as a lever arm for the quadriceps and helps the knee joint to straighten. Patellar tendonitis (also called jumper's knee) is frequently caused by sports that involve repetitive running or jumping, most often basketball. In other teen athletes, the injury may result from general overuse of the knee.

The classic symptom of patellar tendonitis is pain in the lower part of the kneecap that gets worse during running or jumping. In more severe cases, the pain may also be felt while sitting or climbing stairs.

To diagnose patellar tendonitis, your doctor will ask a lot of questions and perform a physical examination. Treatment will first involve rest (particularly the avoidance of all jumping activities) and anti-inflammatory medications as needed. You may also try stretching and strengthening exercises for your quadriceps muscles, as well as ice massage. Surgery is rarely prescribed for patellar tendonitis, but if your injury hasn't responded to nonsurgical treatments in six months, it may be considered.

Return to play following patellar tendonitis varies greatly but usually takes at least a few weeks. Some athletes return to play sooner by using a special knee brace called a patellar tendon strap. In the rare event that surgery is required, return to play may take six months or longer. This injury often returns, requiring repetitive treatment.

PATELLAR SUBLUXATION/INSTABILITY AND DISLOCATION

The patellofemoral joint—knee joint—can become unstable due to an acute mishap (for instance, a direct hit in football or a twisting motion in basketball or running) or from recurrent dislocations or subluxations. Patellofemoral instability is particularly common in teenage athletes, especially in girls.

Patellar dislocation is a distinct event that occurs acutely, often without any contact, and incapacitates the athlete suddenly. Someone who suffers a patellar dislocation may recall the knee "giving out," or hearing a popping sound. Following a dislocation, there will be pain on the inner part of the knee joint, right on the edge of the patella (kneecap). If the dislocation is severe, the kneecap may move out of its groove, causing a fracture of the patella or damage to the cartilage in either the underside of the patella or part of the femur beneath it (this is called an osteochondral fracture).

To diagnose a patellar dislocation, your doctor will perform a physical examination and possibly order an X-ray or MRI.

In most cases, treatment for acute patellar dislocation will involve two weeks of immobilization followed by a rehabilitation program to strengthen the hip muscles and quadriceps. Depending on the nature of the injury, surgery may be necessary, especially in cases of *osteochondral fractures* (cartilage injuries) or significant tearing.

Return to play following instability of the patellofemoral joint varies depending on the degree of soft-tissue damage. If no surgery is required, return to play may take nearly three months, with a patellar-stabilizing brace worn during initial activity. In cases where surgery is necessary, return to play may take much longer. Athletes who have suffered an injury that leads to patellofemoral instability are likely to reinjure the area, so they should take special precautions in the future.

PATELLAR TENDON RUPTURE

Although patellar tendon ruptures are rare in teenagers, they do happen, and when they do, immediate treatment is very important. If it goes untreated, a patellar tendon rupture can be permanently disabling.

Patellar tendon ruptures usually occur acutely, often after an athlete lands on a flexed knee after a jump. Most patellar tendon ruptures take place in knees that are already stressed, however; over time, the tendon degenerates and eventually tears.

Symptoms of a patellar tendon rupture include pain and swelling, particularly at the back of the knee, and the inability to extend (straighten) the knee or bear weight on the affected leg.

To diagnose a patellar tendon rupture, your doctor will perform a physical examination and possibly order an X-ray or MRI. If a patellar tendon rupture is confirmed, treatment will consist of surgery to repair the rupture. After surgery, rehabilitation will involve crutches to keep weight off your knee and a brace worn for up to six weeks to prevent the knee from bending. Once the brace is removed, you should perform exercises to help strengthen your quadriceps muscles. The patellar tendon heals slowly, so return to play following a rupture usually takes six to 12 months.

KNEE FRACTURE

There are a few different types of fractures that can take place in the knee, the most common being a patellar fracture. The patella (kneecap) is almost always fractured because of a direct blow to the knee. Patellar fractures can occur in any sport, and they usually take players out for a significant amount of time, sometimes for the whole season.

Symptoms of a patellar fracture include immediate pain, swelling, reduced motion in the knee, and difficulty bearing weight on the leg. If you suspect a patellar fracture, head to the emergency room. There a physical examination and X-ray will let you know if you have indeed fractured your patella. The X-ray should be interpreted by someone who is very familiar with kneecaps; in some people, the kneecap naturally forms in two pieces that never fuse together, which can be misinterpreted as a fracture. The physician might also take an X-ray of the other (uninjured) kneecap for comparison to assist in the diagnosis.

Treatment of a patellar fracture will depend on the severity of the injury. If the patella isn't too badly misaligned, four to six weeks of immobilization in a brace followed by physical therapy to restore strength, flexibility, and knee function may do the trick. In more severe cases, surgery will be required, also followed by immobilization and physical therapy.

Return to play following a patellar fracture will take at least eight weeks. If you play a contact sport such as football, it could take up to three or four months. In order to get back in the game, you will have to demonstrate good strength and range of motion in your knee.

ANTERIOR CRUCIATE LIGAMENT (ACL) TEAR

When an athlete hurts his or her knee, one of the first things most people will wonder is, "Is it the ACL?" Rupture of the *anterior cruciate ligament* (ACL) is a serious knee injury that involves a tear in the ligament that runs from the top to the bottom of the knee joint, essentially holding the joint together. As increasingly more teenagers engage in sports, ACL injuries are becoming more common in this age group. ACL tears have been found to be more common in females than in males. Sports that put athletes most at risk for an ACL tear are noncontact sports that involve cutting and pivoting, such as soccer, basketball, and hockey. The injury tends to occur when an athlete is rotating the knee when he or she is hit, or if the force of the blow is particularly hard. ACL tears due to direct contact do occur, however, usually in football.

Symptoms of an ACL tear include a loud popping sound as the ligament ruptures, sudden pain and instability in the knee, and rapid swelling (the ACL bleeds quite a bit when it tears). In most cases, an athlete who suffers an ACL tear will fall down and grab his or her knee in pain. The pain may subside quickly, but the feeling of instability and weakness in your knee will remain, especially when you try to put weight on your leg. The knee will also probably become very swollen.

If you suspect an ACL tear, seek immediate medical attention. Your doctor will perform a physical examination and probably order an MRI to see whether the ligament is stretched or completely torn. (X-rays usually aren't very helpful in the diagnosis of an ACL tear.)

Treatment for an ACL injury will depend on a few different factors, including your age, your sport, whether the tear is complete or partial, and whether or not you have additional knee injuries. Nonsurgical treatments, which are usually reserved for a partial ACL tear, include physical therapy to restore strength and range of motion in the knee, and a derotational brace worn during return to play. Surgery is often required in teenagers who play sports; luckily, there have been recent advances in arthroscopic ACL procedures that make the surgery a lot easier than it once was. Physical therapy is often prescribed before surgery to strengthen the knee. Postsurgical care will include crutches for one to two weeks and physical therapy to strengthen the knee, hamstring, quadriceps, and hip.

If you plan to undergo ACL reconstruction surgery, you have many options, all of which involve a graft—tissue transferred from one area (or person) to another. One common procedure is the patellar tendon graft, during which the surgeon cuts out a piece of your patellar tendon and uses it to replace the torn ACL. Some surgeons use the hamstring tendon in a similar manner. Your surgeon might also offer a true ACL graft, taken from a cadaver (the dead body of a human being). Although this procedure is quite effective, many athletes are concerned about the very small risk of transmission of infections such as HIV and hepatitis. While this risk does exist, it is minimized by screening the donors and using radiation on the graft to kill any possible infections.

In athletes who undergo surgery for an ACL tear (which is most athletes), return to play usually takes about six months or longer. When you first return to your sport following the injury, wearing a knee brace may help, depending on your personal preference and whether or not you have any remaining instability in your knee. In order to return to play, you must be able to demonstrate to your doctor that you can perform activities such as cutting, running, twisting, and jumping without pain.

POSTERIOR CRUCIATE LIGAMENT (PCL) INJURY

Posterior cruciate ligament (PCL) injuries are rare. When they do occur, PCL injuries usually result from a head-on blow to the knee during a fall onto a flexed knee, after trauma to the front part of an extended knee, or when the knee is hyperextended. PCL injuries frequently result when a baseball runner slides into the catcher. Other sports that put athletes at risk for PCL injuries are contact sports such as football and sports that require cutting, and pivoting, such as basketball.

PCL injuries differ from ACL injuries in that in many cases the athlete thinks the injury is mild and immediately returns to play only to discover the severity of the injury later, when the pain fails to subside. Symptoms of a PCL injury include pain and swelling in the knee and an inability to run fast without severe pain. A doctor will diagnose a PCL injury with an MRI.

In most cases, PCL injuries respond to nonsurgical treatments such as rest and rehabilitation. The goal of rehabilitation is to strengthen the quadriceps muscles to give support to a knee weakened by a deficient PCL. In rare cases, surgery may be required.

If no surgery is necessary, you will probably be able to return to play following three to six months of rehabilitation. If surgery is required, return to play can take up to six months. Similar to recovery from an ACL tear, athletes can return to play following a PCL injury when they can complete a series of functional tests and run, twist, and jump without pain.

MEDICAL COLLATERAL LIGAMENT (MCL) INJURY

The *medial collateral ligament* is a tight band of tissue that spans the knee joint on the inner side of the knee. MCL injuries usually result from a blow to the knee that forces the knee inward into the knock-kneed position or a twisting of the knee that causes the same motion. Sports that typically lead to an MCL tear include football, soccer, and skiing.

Symptoms of an MCL tear may include an audible pop, a feeling of tearing in the knee, pain on the inside of the knee at the upper part of the joint, and limited range of motion.

To diagnose an MCL tear, your doctor will perform a physical examination and possibly order an MRI (mostly to rule out an ACL or meniscus injury). Most athletes with a significant MCL injury are in a great deal of pain and are unable to walk without a significant limp. Therefore, initial treatment often involves a knee immobilizer, which offers temporary comfort and support. Because it prevents the knee from bending, this immobilizer can lead to stiffness and weakness, so it's important to move your knee as soon as your physician says it's OK. There are also other braces available that can provide some support while still allowing your knee to bend and your muscles to work.

Luckily, most MCL injuries can be treated successfully without surgery. If the injury is mild, initial treatment will involve ice at least twice a day for 20 minutes at a time, exercises to strengthen the quadriceps, and stationary cycling if it can be done without pain. In some cases, supervised physical therapy will be necessary. Continuing to move the knee to keep it from stiffening is an important part of recovery.

If the tear is more severe, treatment will involve a period of bracing for four to six weeks to help the ligament heal in combination with physical therapy. If other ligaments are involved, surgery may be required.

Depending on its severity, return to play following an MCL injury may take several months. In order to return to play, you must be pain-free and have restored the original strength and range of motion in your knee.

LATERAL COLLATERAL LIGAMENT (LCL) TEAR/SPRAIN

The *lateral collateral ligament* (LCL) is the counterpart to the medial collateral ligament—it is a tight band of tissue that travels up the *outside* of the knee. Isolated LCL injuries are uncommon and usually result from a blow to the inner side of the knee toward the outer side—typically a blow during a contact sport such as football or a specific stress applied during wrestling.

An isolated LCL injury can usually be treated without surgery. If multiple ligaments are affected, however, surgery may be necessary.

Return to play following an LCL injury may take several weeks, depending on how quickly you can restore range of motion and eliminate pain. Once you do return to play, you will probably have to wear a knee sleeve with supports on both the inner and outer portions of your knee.

POSTEROLATERAL CORNER INJURIES

The *posterolateral corner* is a junction of muscles and ligaments in the knee that help it flex. Sports injuries to the posterolateral corner usually result from a blow to the inner side of the back of the knee when the knee is extended.

Symptoms of a posterolateral corner injury include pain in the knee coupled with a sensation that the knee is "giving out" when you are walking. There may also be tenderness at the top of the fibula and bruising in the area.

To diagnose a posterolateral corner injury, your doctor will perform a physical examination, often coupled with an MRI.

Treatment for a posterolateral corner injury will depend on the severity of the problem. If the injury is mild, your doctor may prescribe a brace and rehabilitation exercises. If it is more severe, surgery may be in order.

Return to play following a posterolateral corner injury will vary depending on the severity. In some cases, an athlete can get right back to his or her sport; in other cases, it may take several months for the injury to heal.

MENISCUS INJURIES

The meniscus is a piece of cartilage in the knee located at the junction of the two bones in the knee joint. Meniscal tears (also called "torn cartilage" or a "locked knee") can happen at any age. In teenagers, they usually result from a traumatic injury to the knee, often when the knee twists while the foot is in a fixed position. More meniscal tears take place on the medial (inside) part of the knee than on the lateral (outside) portion, but both injuries are caused by a twisting motion of the leg. Basketball, football, and soccer most often lead to meniscus injuries.

Symptoms of a meniscus injury may be vague but usually include pain and swelling in the knee, often following a painful popping or tearing sensation that typically occurs due to a twisting motion. At first, the pain and swelling may be incapacitating, making it impossible for you to bend or straighten your knee. Symptoms will probably gradually improve with time, though the pain may get worse when you rotate your leg, walk down stairs, or strike a particular position while sleeping. You may also hear a clicking sound when you rotate your knee.

To diagnose a meniscal tear, your doctor will perform a physical examination and most likely order an MRI to confirm the diagnosis.

Depending on the severity of the injury and whether the knee is continuously locked, treatment for a meniscal tear may require surgery. Blood circulation to the meniscus is limited, so healing occurs very slowly. Surgery, which may be used to repair the meniscus or remove the torn fragment, is done arthroscopically, and many patients return to full knee function in as little as six weeks. Physical therapy or a home exercise program can help to speed healing.

When surgery is not required, treatment will include immobilization (crutches) followed by four to six weeks in a brace. You may be able to return to play in about eight to 12 weeks. If surgery is performed, you might even return sooner—as early as four weeks following the injury. When you do return to your sport, you should progress slowly and stop whenever you feel pain.

OSGOOD-SCHLATTER SYNDROME

Osgood-Schlatter syndrome is a painful condition that affects growing children and teenagers. The pain comes from the growth plate of the bump on the leg just below the kneecap, called the tibial tubercle. Once the growth plate closes—which happens at an earlier age in females (usually at 16) than males (around 17)—symptoms should disappear.

Symptoms of Osgood-Schlatter syndrome, which may include tenderness, swelling, and warmth on the tibial tubercle, are caused by running and jumping activities.

Osgood-Schlatter syndrome is initially diagnosed in growing teenage athletes. In rare cases, adults with the disease may continue to have pain on the tibial tubercle when a small piece of bone (called an unfused ossicle) persists in the area.

There is also a condition similar to Osgood-Schlatter syndrome called Sinding-Larsen-Johansson disease. The only difference between these two syndromes is that in the case of Sinding-Larsen-Johansson disease, the inflammation occurs closer to the point where the patellar tendon attaches to the kneecap.

Years ago, children and teenagers with Osgood-Schlatter syndrome or Sinding-Larsen-Johansson disease were banned from sports.

Today, however, most cases can be treated without surgery. Treatment is aimed at minimizing pain with rest, stretching, strengthening exercises, and possibly seven days of anti-inflammatory medication. Immobilization may also be helpful in some cases. In patients who have a remaining unfused ossicle in the knee, however, surgery may be required to remove it.

Return to play following treatment for Osgood-Schlatter syndrome or Sinding-Larsen-Johansson disease depends on the severity of symptoms and how much they interfere with the sufferer's ability to play his or her sport. Luckily, the condition will resolve itself by age 16 or 17, regardless of treatment.

STRESS FRACTURES

If you stress anything over and over, it will eventually crack and break. Think about a stick—if you bend it repeatedly, it's only a matter of time until it snaps in half. Like that stick, the bones in your legs can weaken and crack under the stress of repeated pounding. Both the tibia and fibula in the lower leg are bones vulnerable to stress fractures, but tibial stress fractures are much more common because the tibia is a major weight-bearing bone. Certain risk factors such as osteoporosis, a sudden increase in training, an eating disorder, or an improper diet can all put you at a higher risk for stress fractures, but even normal bones will eventually break if they are put under abnormal stress. Biomechanical issues can actually place uneven stresses on your bones during exercise and result in a stress fracture. Females are at particular risk for stress fractures when they miss their periods as a result of inadequate dietary intake.

In the early stages of a stress fracture, when the bone is damaged but not yet cracked (called a stress reaction), there may be slight pain or no pain at all. Once the bone cracks, the pain will increase dramatically, and you will be able to pinpoint it down to a single finger's width on your lower leg. The pain will also go from only occurring when you exercise to persisting when you perform other daily activities. You may also notice a small tender bump along the bone, indicating that it is trying to heal itself.

To diagnose a stress fracture, your doctor will perform a physical examination and order an X-ray, then probably follow up with an MRI or bone scan. X-rays of stress fractures usually appear normal unless the fracture has been there for a month or more. In severe cases, a stress fracture may progress to the point that the bone breaks all the way through (in which case it will show up on an X-ray—known in medicine as the "dreaded black line"), but this is rare. If you are a female with a stress fracture, your doctor may also screen you for the female athlete triad, which consists of an eating disorder (the lack of adequate dietary intake mentioned above), amenorrhea (absence of a menstrual period), and osteoporosis.

Treatment for a stress fracture involves anti-inflammatory medications and rest to allow the bone to heal. If the pain is severe, your doctor may also prescribe crutches or a bone stimulator (a device that assists in the laying down of new bone, speeding the healing process). If your doctor suspects the female athlete triad, he or she may also send you for psychological counseling.

Stress fractures usually take as long to heal as you've been exercising with pain. In some teenage athletes, this may mean three to six months. Most athletes with stress fractures of the lower leg can engage in some form of cross training (such as weight lifting, cycling, elliptical training, or deep-water running) as the fracture heals.

MEDIAL TIBIAL STRESS SYNDROME (SHIN SPLINTS)

If you are a runner, surely you or one of your teammates has uttered the phrase, "I think I have shin splints." This catchall term, used frequently by coaches and runners alike to label any pain on the inner side of the shin, usually describes *medial tibial stress syndrome.* In the case of medial tibial stress syndrome, the sleeve of tissue surrounding the tibia becomes inflamed due to repeated stress.

The more common types of shin splints are actually pains in the muscle beside the shin bone. Both types of shin splints are caused by running, jumping, or other forms of overuse. Shin splints usually occur in people who are not used to training, but they can also affect athletes who step up their training regimens, get new shoes, start running on harder surfaces, or start speed workouts. Shin splints may also strike athletes who have biomechanical imbalances anywhere from the back or pelvis all the way down to the feet.

Symptoms of shin splints include burning or aching on the inner part of the shin after activity. The pain usually spreads out over an area of three-fingers width along the front or back edge of the shin bone.

To diagnose shin splits, your doctor will perform a physical examination and may order a bone scan or MRI to rule out a stress fracture. (X-rays usually appear normal in the case of shin splints, so they aren't used in the diagnosis.)

Treatment for shin splints involves correcting the problem that led to the injury in the first place. This may include a decrease in mileage, frequency, and intensity. If the pain persists despite pulling back, you will need to seek further medical attention to rule out a stress fracture or compartment syndrome. If your feet overpronate (roll inward), your doctor may also prescribe athletic inserts or custom orthotics for your running shoes.

Following shin splints, you will probably be able to get back on the track, cross-country course, or field after a week or two of rest—as soon as you can run comfortably again.

CHRONIC EXERTIONAL COMPARTMENT SYNDROME

Muscles in the lower leg are surrounded by thick, fibrous tissues that form tubes called compartments. These compartments are tight—they don't allow overdeveloped muscles much room to expand. When you exercise, as your lower leg muscles become engorged with blood, the pressure of the muscles against the surrounding compartments doesn't allow blood to escape. As a result, blood continues to enter the muscles and pools there, putting pressure on the compartments. Eventually, this pressure builds up until blood from the arteries can no longer get into the muscle. Without blood (and therefore, oxygen), the muscles can become damaged and may even die.

Because its symptoms mimic so many other lower leg injuries, compartment syndrome is somewhat hard to diagnose. Symptoms include pain, swelling, and sensitivity in the affected muscular compartment, often accompanied by numbness or tingling in the feet. The pain and discomfort usually increase during the course of a workout and improve shortly afterward.

Unfortunately, compartment syndrome doesn't usually show up on X-rays or other imaging studies. Therefore, to accurately diagnose compartment syndrome, your doctor may have to inject a local anesthetic and then measure the pressure in your lower leg compartments by inserting a needle while you exercise.

Treatment for compartment syndrome first involves rest. If that fails to work, surgery may be necessary to reduce pressure in the affected compartment.

Return to play following compartment syndrome will depend on whether or not surgery is part of the treatment. If you don't need surgery, you will be able to return to play as soon as you can walk and run without pain (you can test for this on a treadmill). If you've had surgery, however, it will likely be several weeks before you are able to return to your sport.

ACUTE TIBIAL AND FIBULAR FRACTURES

Acute tibial and fibular fractures usually result from a fall or hard blow to the lower leg. Both fractures are medical emergencies that require immediate treatment.

Frequently seen in skiers, tibial fractures are also called "boot-top" fractures because the leg breaks where the top of a ski boot would reach. Tibial fractures are particularly serious because the tibia is a weight-bearing bone and also tends to heal slowly and poorly due to the lack of blood supply to the area. Return to play following a tibial fracture often takes several months.

Acute fibular fractures are usually less serious because the fibula isn't a weight-bearing bone, but they still require emergency medical treatment. In most cases, an athlete with a fibular fracture can return to play in about four to five weeks.

PREVENTING KNEE AND LOWER LEG INJURIES

Unfortunately, as a teen athlete, there isn't much you can do to prevent knee and lower leg injuries; by virtue of playing sports, you put yourself at risk. Exercises to strengthen and stretch your quadriceps muscles and your hips (see pp. 116 and 132) can help, as may knee braces that help stabilize the joint. The goal of strengthening exercises is to improve lower extremity and core muscle fitness, thus helping you to avoid positions that put you at a greater risk for lower leg and knee injuries. You may also want to have your biomechanics analyzed by a physical therapist or your school trainer. For example, if you are a runner, your gait may put you at risk for knee injuries, and changing it only slightly may go far in prevention. In addition, try the following:

> ➤ If you are a runner, try to keep your weekly mileage to less than 40 miles.
> ➤ Avoid increasing mileage more than 10 percent per week.
> ➤ Avoid running on hard, uneven, or slippery surfaces whenever you can.
> ➤ Get properly fitted for the shoes you wear during your sport. Since your foot can widen, make sure you are professionally fitted each time you buy a new pair.

> If you overpronate (your feet roll in), consider athletic inserts or getting fitted for orthotics.
> Put shock-absorbing soft insoles in your shoes to help prevent stress fractures.

STRETCHING AND STRENGTHENING EXERCISES FOR THE KNEE

Toe raise. Stand with your feet together. Rise up on your toes for 10 seconds, then come down flat on the floor. Repeat until your calf muscles feel fatigued. As your calf muscles begin to get stronger, put all of your weight on your affected leg and keep the other leg off the floor. Then hold dumbbells to increase your body weight.

Wall sit. Stand about two feet in front of a wall (smoother wall is better) and lean your back flush against it. Slide down until your knees approach but do not exceed 90-degree angles (choose an angle within this range that is comfortable for you) and hold, keeping the abs contracted, for 10 to 60 seconds. Return to starting position and repeat. Three to five sets of 30 seconds each is a good starting point for most athletes, but this may vary.

Heel drop. Stand with the front of your feet on a raised surface such as a book (as if you were going to do a back dive off a diving board). Let your weight take your heels down below the level of the surface in order to stretch your calf muscles. Hold for 10 to 15 seconds, then come back up. Repeat until your calves are fatigued.

Straight leg raise. Lie down on your back with one leg bent and one leg straight. Push your belly button toward the floor so your back is flat against the floor/mat. With your toes pointed to the ceiling, keep your knee straight and lift your leg up to about 45 degrees, no higher than the bent knee. Slowly lower your leg back to the floor and repeat 10 to 15 times. Do three sets if possible.

Side-to-side shuffle. Get into a squatting position with your arms bent in front of you and your elbows by your sides. Shuffle 10 to 15 feet to your right, moving your right foot, then your left foot. Then return the other way, leading with your left foot. Repeat 10 times on each side.

Lunge. Stand with your feet shoulder-width apart and hold two dumbbells in your hands with your arms down by your sides. Step forward with one leg so there is about two to 2.5 feet between your feet. Lower your upper body down, bending your front leg so that your thigh is parallel to the ground and your shin is perpendicular to the ground. Do not allow your knee to go forward beyond your toes as you come down. Push back and repeat with the other leg. Do 10 repetitions on each side.

Standing quad stretch. Stand with your feet shoulder-width apart. Grab the foot of your affected leg and gently pull your heel toward your buttocks, bending your knee. Feel the stretch in the front of your leg and hold for five seconds. Repeat 10 times.

Hamstring stretch. Lie on your back with your feet flat on the floor and your knees bent. Bend the hip of one leg, grasp your thigh just behind your knee, and slowly straighten your knee until you feel tightness behind your knee. Hold for five seconds, then relax. Repeat with the other leg. If you don't feel the stretch, bend your hip a little more and repeat.

Iliotibial band (ITB) stretch. Lie on one side, then lift your upper leg toward the ceiling. From this position, rotate your upper foot outward toward the ceiling and bring this entire leg backward behind your body. Then allow this upper leg to drop slowly until you feel a stretch along the outer thigh. Hold 20 to 30 seconds and repeat three times. Repeat on the other side.

Isometric quad exercise. While sitting in a chair, fully extend your leg and tighten your quad muscle to pull your kneecap up. Hold for one second, then relax. Repeat 50 times, several times a day. If this exercise is painful, try doing it with your leg slightly flexed.

WHAT YOU NEED TO KNOW

▶ Most knee pain is the result of an acute or chronic injury. However, it is also important to rule out causes of pain that may not be the result of sports activity, including infection, arthritis, referred pain from the hip (i.e., Perthes disease), or malignancy.

▶ Athletes who have suffered knee injuries are likely to experience a recurrence, so they should take special precautions to protect their knees.

➤ If you suspect a patellar fracture, head to the emergency room. Symptoms include immediate pain, swelling, reduced motion in the knee, and difficulty bearing weight on the leg.

➤ Symptoms of an ACL tear include a loud popping sound as the ligament ruptures, sudden pain and instability in the knee, and rapid swelling (the ACL bleeds quite a bit when it tears). If you suspect an ACL tear, seek immediate medical attention.

10

Foot and Ankle Injuries

Will, 16, is a sophomore on his high school cross-country team. In his freshman year, Will was one of the top runners on the men's team. Now that he is a sophomore, Will really wants to excel. Unfortunately, during his last meet, Will caught his foot on a rock, his foot rolled over his toes, and he fell to the ground. Will felt his ankle twist and pull as he fell, and he was immediately on the side of the course, writhing in pain. Within minutes, his ankle was bruised and very swollen.

A few hours later, at the hospital, Will learned that he had suffered a *high ankle sprain*—an injury to the large ligament above the ankle that joins together the two bones of the lower leg. Will did the right thing by seeking treatment right away—because they can quickly worsen, ankle injuries shouldn't be taken lightly.

The good news is that although Will will have to refrain from running for six weeks or so and probably use crutches while the sprain heals, he is likely to recover from the injury completely. His ankle may be more vulnerable to sprains in the future, however, so he will have to be careful.

In addition to ankle sprains, this chapter will cover some of the most common injuries of the foot and ankle and offer advice on how teen athletes can best prevent and treat those injuries.

THE ANKLE

The ankle is designed to help your foot move in many directions—up and down so you can walk, and from the inside and outside so you

135

can adjust to uneven surfaces or walk on the side of a hill. But all this motion puts the ankle at risk for injury, particularly in teens who play sports.

There are two main types of acute ankle injuries—sprains and fractures. Although they are very different injuries, both sprains and fractures cause swelling and bruising. An ankle with only minimal swelling may be broken, while one with significant swelling may only be sprained. For this reason, you should seek medical attention for any injury to your ankle, especially if you feel pain on the inside of the joint. This may involve getting an X-ray. If you go down suddenly and severely injure your ankle, the area should be splinted until you get to the emergency room.

ANKLE SPRAIN

Ankle sprains are extremely common in the United States, accounting for one out of 10 visits to the emergency room. Most of these sprains result from contact sports or sports that involve pivoting, such as basketball.

There are three grades of ankle sprains—grades 1, 2, and 3. In the case of a mild grade 1 sprain, the ankle twists only slightly, stretching the ligament—for example, when you twist your ankle gently after stepping off a curb. A moderate grade 2 sprain, which involves partial tearing of the fibers of the ligament, may result from a harder twist—for example, when a tennis player lunges out over a poorly planted foot. In the case of a severe grade 3 sprain, most or all of the fibers tear, making the ankle very loose and unstable.

In addition to the three different grades, there are a few different types of ankle sprains—for our purposes, lateral (outer) sprains, medial (inner) sprains, and high ankle sprains.

The most common type of an ankle sprain is a *lateral ankle sprain* (also called an inversion sprain)—a sprain of the ligaments on the outside of your ankle—caused by rolling onto the outer part of the ankle joint. Symptoms of a lateral sprain include swelling and pain on the outer area of the ankle and bruising around the injury. A few days later, your foot and toes may also become bruised.

Medial ankle sprains (also called eversion sprains), which result from rolling off the inside of your foot, are much less common than lateral sprains. In fact, this motion very often leads to a fracture rather than a sprain. With a medial sprain, the inside ligament is stressed, and in many cases, rather than becoming sprained itself, it pulls off a piece of bone where it attaches. This is because it is such a strong ligament. Medial sprains typically require an X-ray for diagnosis.

The third type of ankle sprain, which often occurs in addition to the injuries mentioned above is called a high ankle sprain. With a high ankle sprain, the large ligament above the ankle that joins together the two bones of the lower leg becomes injured. High ankle sprains are often more severe, and they can take much longer to heal.

As mentioned above, you should seek medical attention for any type of ankle injury. In the meantime, treat your ankle with RICE to eliminate internal bleeding and swelling. The intense pain of a sprained ankle eases rather quickly, so you may be tempted to get back in the game, but you should resist this temptation. If the pain is severe, you may want to splint your ankle until you can be treated. Continue to ice the injury for 20 minutes or until it starts to feel numb, then take the ice off for another 20 minutes. Keep icing on and off for 20 minutes at a time for a total of 48 hours, or until the ankle returns to its normal size. Use compression in between icings and at night while you sleep, elevating your ankle above your heart whenever you can.

Your doctor should be able to diagnose a sprain and tell you which grade you've suffered and may get an X-ray or MRI if needed. Treatment will involve continuing RICE and possibly an ankle stirrup brace to support the ligaments. Range-of-motion exercises are typically started, once tolerated, to reduce stiffness and restore mobility. When you're ready, a more advanced strengthening program should follow, either at home or at physical therapy. Depending on the severity of the sprain, your treatment may initially require crutches. If you suffer persistent sprains, surgery may also be necessary.

Overall, ankle sprains should not be ignored. Do not push through pain with this injury, if you do, you may cause a worse sprain. Instead, while your ankle is healing, maintain your cardiovascular fitness with "safe" activities such as stationary cycling or deepwater running, as tolerated and as allowed by your doctor.

Athletes with ankle sprains are usually allowed to return to play once they are able to run through drills that resemble the sport without pain (sometimes in a brace or taping for added support). For example, many physicians will ask a football or soccer player to run a "figure 8" before returning to play. Timing depends on the grade and location of the injury. Grade 1 sprains may take only one to two weeks to heal, while grade 2 and grade 3 sprains take four to six weeks or even longer in some cases.

To prevent a future ankle sprain after your ankle has healed—which is more likely once you've sprained your ankle the first time—make sure it is as strong and stable as possible. If not, then at the very least you should wrap your ankle tightly in athletic tape or use a lace-up cloth ankle brace. If it is still weak, consider using an

Air Cast, which will hold your ankle up firmly until it has completely restrengthened.

If you have a problem with recurring sprains, you can try using a special brace (prescribed by your doctor) to prevent your heel from turning over.

BROKEN ANKLE

Unfortunately, broken ankles occur fairly often in teens who play sports. A basketball player jumps to make a shot and lands hard on the side of another player's foot. A soccer player digs a foot into the ground at the same time another player steps on his or her ankle. Or a baseball player slides into home and on the way catches his cleats in the dirt. All of these activities can lead to a broken ankle.

A broken ankle can be fairly difficult to recognize, as the signs may closely mimic an ankle sprain. Symptoms include swelling and pain that get worse after exercise, bruising in the ankle, and limited range of motion. The pain may be intermixed with pain-free periods, or it may take the form of a dull ache that never quite goes away.

Ankle fractures can take a few different forms, from a small chip to a complex fracture that requires surgery. All types of ankle fractures require medical attention, however. Treatment will either involve a cast or surgery and will also include a rehabilitation program to help strengthen your ankle. In many cases, a broken ankle requires treatment by an orthopedic surgeon.

The time it takes to return to play following a broken ankle will depend on your sport, the type of fracture, and how fast you can restore 100 percent strength and range of motion in the area. Practicing or competing on a weakened ankle will only lead to another injury, so taking the time for adequate healing is essential. If you are a runner, you will probably be able to get back on the track or course in about three to four months, sometimes sooner. If you participate in a pivoting sport, it will take longer—perhaps four to six months.

ACHILLES TENDONITIS

The most common cause of Achilles tendonitis, or the inflammation of the Achilles tendon, appears to be not warming up and stretching properly before sports practice or play. Achilles tendonitis can occur in different locations—typically either within the tendon itself or at the insertion of the tendon into the heel (called Haglund's disease).

Symptoms of Achilles tendonitis include a tender, swollen, and painful Achilles tendon and sometimes chronic pain in the lower back part of the calf muscle. The tendon may also develop a painful lump that can be felt if you pinch it between your fingers.

To diagnose Achilles tendonitis, your doctor will perform a physical examination. Unfortunately, the healing process is long and slow, and because Achilles tendonitis usually occurs in people who are very active, it can be a frustrating wait. Treatment involves resting the tendon by refraining from exercise, physical therapy, and in some cases, wearing shoes with a slightly elevated heel to avoid further stretching until it is ready. Even after Achilles tendonitis has healed, a small, firm lump often remains.

Return to play following Achilles tendonitis can't take place until the pain is completely gone. Once you've returned to your sport, you should continue physical therapy and stretching exercises to prevent reinjury.

ACHILLES TENDON RUPTURE

While mostly seen in "weekend warrior" athletes more than 30 years old, an Achilles tendon rupture may occur in teens, usually resulting from pre-existing tendonitis in the Achilles tendon or inadequate stretching before activity. Achilles tendon ruptures are fairly rare, but when they do occur, they usually result from sports that involve pivoting or twisting, such as football, soccer, racquet sports, and basketball.

Symptoms of an Achilles tendon rupture include a popping sensation at the back of the ankle (often described as feeling as if you were smacked there), a gap that can be felt at the back of the tendon, and a loss of motion in the ankle. If you've suffered an Achilles tendon rupture, you will not be able to actively flex your ankle downward (as if you were stepping on the gas pedal in a car). Because of the severe pain, you probably won't be able to bear weight on the affected leg.

If you think you've ruptured your Achilles tendon, seek medical attention as soon as possible. In the meantime, use RICE.

To diagnose a rupture, your physician will examine your Achilles tendon. Unfortunately, many partial Achilles tendon ruptures are missed even by trained professionals, so it is helpful if your physician has experience in diagnosing this type of injury.

Treatment for a ruptured Achilles tendon may be surgical or nonsurgical. If your physician opts for the nonsurgical route, you will wear a cast or special boot with your foot held in the foot-down position until the tendon heals, usually for about six to eight weeks. Although this method avoids surgery, there is a risk of rupturing the tendon again during the healing period. Surgery is effective at restoring the normal length and function of the tendon, but it carries the risk of wound infections and phlebitis. Together, you and your physician can weigh the pros and cons of each method and determine what's best for you.

Whether or not your treatment involves surgery, you will need to perform exercises to restrengthen your Achilles tendon before you return to your sport.

Return to play following an Achilles tendon rupture depends on the sport you play. You can usually begin running about four months following the injury and start pivoting sports at about six months. In extreme cases, it may be up to a year before an athlete can return to play following an Achilles tendon rupture.

THE FOOT

Your feet are two of the most important and complex parts of your body. Made up of 26 bones and soft tissues, your feet absorb the shock of your body's weight during activity, provide a stable base for your body, and act as levers to propel your body forward while you walk. At no time are these actions more important than during sports play. When you sprint, your feet absorb up to four times your body weight. If you dive off a diving board, your feet must bend and lock into a rigid position so you can push off from your toes. If you play football, your feet will roll from the outside to the inside as you propel forward during a tackle.

Because feet are such an important part of sports performance, any foot abnormality will literally throw you off balance. Many overuse injuries in the lower legs, hips, and back are due to an anomaly in the feet or the way they hit the ground during activity. One way to prevent these problems is by properly aligning the foot (sometimes with the aid of an orthotic).

Common foot abnormalities include excessive pronation, a foot that rolls too far inward; supination, a foot that rolls outward; *Morton's foot,* a second toe that is longer than the first toe; and pes planus (flat feet), which are feet that do not have an adequate arch.

But whether or not there is a foot abnormality causing an injury elsewhere on the body, some athletes experience pain directly on the foot, which can be caused by a number of different injuries. Here are some of the most common:

LISFRANC INJURIES

A Lisfranc injury is an injury to the mid-foot, where a cluster of small bones forms an arch on top of the foot. Although there is some connective tissue in the foot, there is no connective tissue between the first metatarsal (big toe) and the second metatarsal (second toe). Therefore, a twist to the foot can push these bones out of place, injuring the adjacent ligament (the *Lisfranc complex*), which functions to hold these bones together. Lisfranc injuries commonly result from car or motorcycle accidents or an accidental step into a small hole.

Symptoms of a Lisfranc injury are often similar to those of an ankle sprain, but the pain is experienced in the mid-foot. Symptoms include bruising, and in severe cases, an inability to put weight on the affected foot.

To diagnose a Lisfranc injury, your doctor will conduct a physical examination and perhaps order an X-ray. Lisfranc injuries are often tough to see on X-rays, however, so your doctor may have to order several views or get an MRI.

Treatment for a Lisfranc injury depends on the severity of the problem. If the bones have not been pushed out of position, treatment will most likely include crutches for six weeks or so. If the bones have been pushed out of position or if there is an associated break in the bone (called a "fracture-dislocation"), surgery may be necessary to hold the bones in place until healing is complete. In both cases, your doctor (usually an orthopedist) will prescribe exercises to help restore strength and range of motion in your foot. Return to play depends on the particular situation, but in general, this injury takes a while to heal, typically at least several weeks. In the meantime, you should avoid any activities that are painful.

BRUISED FOOT

Any sports activity that puts the foot in harm's way, where it can be slammed too hard against a soccer ball, pelted with a baseball, or stepped on by a fellow basketball player, increases the risk of a bruised foot.

Symptoms of a bruised foot include pain and bruising. In most cases, a bruised foot can be treated at home with ice and rest for four to five days until the pain subsides.

PLANTAR FASCIITIS

The *plantar fascia* is an elastic band on the sole of the foot that helps hold up the arch. It runs from the heel bone to the toes, and it helps absorb shock. In teen athletes, particularly runners, the plantar fascia can overstretch or partially tear, leading to pain and inflammation—plantar fasciitis.

Plantar fasciitis often strikes athletes who have high arches (supinators). Symptoms of the injury include pain when putting weight on the foot or pushing off while running or walking. This pain, which results from a plantar fascia that is stretched and torn, is often very intense (described by some as feeling like there is a tack in the heel). The discomfort is at its worst when the foot is stiff after a prolonged period of sitting or lying down, such as in the morning as you get out of bed. Each time you put weight on the foot, the plantar fascia is strained and tears again across your arch.

If you suspect plantar fasciitis, see your doctor. He or she will perform a physical examination to confirm the diagnosis.

With regard to treatment, a study done by the American Orthopedic Foot and Ankle Society found that 90 percent of cases of plantar fasciitis heal within nine months, regardless of treatment—an indication that the most important aspect of treatment is rest. There are, however, some things you can do to speed the process. You can put an arch support under your foot to prevent further stretching and tearing of the plantar fascia. You can also use an arch support in your slippers and avoid walking in bare feet. Other treatment options include a night splint (or special slipper) worn to hold your foot/toes up while you sleep, heel cups, ice ball massage, and physical therapy. If the injury is mild, you should start to feel relief with these measures in just a few days. In severe cases, steroid injections, shock wave therapy, or surgery may be necessary to correct the problem.

Return to play following plantar fasciitis depends on the severity on the injury and can take place only once you are completely pain-free. In some cases, this may only take a few weeks. In others, it could be up to a year. If surgery is necessary, expect return to play to take at least a few months.

STRESS FRACTURE OF THE FOOT (METATARSAL)

In runners and other teenage athletes who ask a lot of their feet, the long, thin bones that run from the top of the foot to the toes—the metatarsal bones—can crack from stress. When your foot flexes during a run, tremendous force is transmitted to the first metatarsal, behind the big toe. If that bone is too short, such as in Morton's foot, your weight will be shifted to the surrounding metatarsal bones, which aren't as thick and can crack more easily. Therefore, the second, third, and forth metatarsal bones are also vulnerable to stress fractures.

A stress fracture that occurs in the middle of the second, third, or fourth metatarsal is called a "march" fracture. Originally named for soldiers who suffered the injury after a long march, today this type of fracture is common in runners who suddenly step up their training regimen, especially those who are training for a marathon. Female ballet dancers are also vulnerable to march fractures because of the weight they put on their toes.

Symptoms of a metatarsal bone stress fracture usually come on gradually, with a nagging pain in the foot during exercise (which usually lasts for a few weeks) followed by a sudden pain in the front part of your foot. In addition, you may experience tenderness and swelling on both the upper and lower surfaces of your foot.

To diagnose a stress fracture of a metatarsal, your doctor will probably order an X-ray, MRI, or a bone scan to confirm the injury. Treatment will primarily involve rest for four to six weeks to allow the bone to heal. This rest may include crutches if you feel severe pain when you walk. Otherwise, your doctor may prescribe a stirrup brace (Air Cast) or walking boot for immobilization. Plaster casts are usually not necessary, but you may need an orthotic to help distribute your weight properly as the fracture heals.

A stress fracture of the fifth metatarsal, which is behind the little toe, is a more serious injury that results from a strain on the outside of the foot. Symptoms include increasing pain on the outer foot associated with activity, and occasionally an audible popping sound with immediate pain, swelling, and discoloration if the bone fully breaks. This type of stress fracture may require a cast and crutches from anywhere from six weeks to several months. In severe cases, surgery may be necessary.

NAVICULAR STRESS FRACTURE

A common foot injury in athletes, navicular stress fractures are stress fractures that take place at the mid-foot just beyond the ankle. As with other stress fractures, they often follow recent increases in training and usually occur in endurance athletes, as well as those who engage in explosive movements as part of their sports (sprinters, basketball players, soccer players, high jumpers, etc).

Symptoms of a navicular stress fracture include vague pain on the top of the foot, just beyond the ankle, sometimes accompanied by swelling. This pain usually worsens after exercise and resolves shortly afterward. If the stress fracture is more severe, the pain may persist during everyday activities.

To diagnose a navicular stress fracture, your doctor will perform a physical examination and probably order an X-ray. Navicular stress fractures are often not seen on X-rays, so a bone scan, CT scan, or MRI is often necessary to make the diagnosis.

Treatment of a navicular stress fracture typically involves a short-leg cast coupled with crutches. In most cases, navicular stress fractures heal in about six weeks, after which athletes can slowly return to play.

FREIBERG INFRACTION

A term first coined by Alfred H. Freiberg in 1914, a *Freiberg infraction* describes a painful collapse of the joint surface of the second metatarsal head (where the second toe meets the foot). The injury usually results from overuse, particularly from running, jumping, or dancing. Freiberg infractions are probably far more common than we realize and can occur in high school athletes. When they do occur, symptoms include pain at the front of the foot, usually in the area of the second toe. The pain may get worse the more time you spend on your feet. The severity of the injury ranges—sometimes it just flares up as a result of activity, and in other cases, the sufferer can't bear weight on the affected foot.

If you have any of these symptoms, see your doctor. Treatment options, which depend on the severity of the injury, include orthotics, inserts, and stiff-soled shoes. Surgery is usually reserved for the most severe cases, when there is a loose body floating in the joint. Return to activity following a Freiberg infraction depends on the seriousness of the injury.

TURF TOE

A violent injury that occurs most often in contact sports such as football, soccer, and basketball, turf toe results when one player steps on another player's foot, driving the phalangeal (big toe) joint upward suddenly and tearing the tendons that attach under the base of the big toe.

Symptoms of turf toe, which is so-named because it is more likely to occur on hard artificial turf, include pain, swelling, bruising, and difficulty bearing weight on the ball of the foot. Turf toe can be graded as 1, 2, or 3 depending on its severity.

Turf toe is a potentially serious injury, and if it isn't treated correctly, it can lead to lifelong disability. As a result, surgery is often necessary. If not, nonsurgical treatments include taping the toe and wearing a special shoe to immobilize the area and speed healing.

Return to play following turf toe will depend on the degree of the injury. In mild cases, it may take only a month, but if the injury is more severe, it could take up to a year to get back in the game.

BLACK TOENAIL

Common in runners, skiers, and tennis players, a black toenail (also called tennis toe) is a bruise under the toenail. It is usually caused by wearing shoes/boots that are too small or by not lacing your shoes/boots tightly enough to hold your foot firmly in the back of your shoe or boot.

Although they are at first very painful, then unsightly and slightly uncomfortable, black toenails are not serious. In the acute setting, your doctor might use a needle (sometimes hot) to poke one or more holes in your nail to release the pressure from the trapped blood that is causing pain. Given enough time, if you replace ill-fitting shoes with shoes that fit you properly, the black toenail will be replaced with a nice new clear one. You should expect this process to take about a year.

SHOELACE PRESSURE SYNDROME

If you tie your shoelaces too tight, or the tongue of your athletic shoes is pushed too snugly against your foot, you may develop shoelace pressure syndrome.

Symptoms of shoelace pressure syndrome include numbness, tingling, or pain at the top of your foot where your shoelaces are tied, all of which may radiate toward your toes.

After your doctor rules out other potential causes of your symptoms, he or she will instruct you to tie your shoelaces more loosely to relieve symptoms. To make sure you buy athletic shoes that fit you properly, shop for them in the afternoon or evening (because your feet swell later in the day and are more likely to be the size they will be during exercise), and wear the same socks you wear during exercise.

GROWTH PLATE INJURIES OF THE FOOT AND ANKLE

Growth plates, also called the epiphyseal plate or physis, are areas of growing tissue at both ends of the long bones of children and teenagers. Growth plates determine the eventual length and shape of the mature bones. When the bone is done growing, the growth plates close and are replaced by solid bone.

Growth plates are the weakest part of the growing skeleton in kids and teenagers, even weaker than the surrounding ligaments and bones. Therefore, a growing teen who experiences a fall or blow during sports play may be more likely to injure a growth plate than to suffer a sprain. Both your feet and your ankles contain growth plates and therefore are vulnerable to growth plate injuries.

Most growth plate injuries are fractures; in fact, they make up about 15 percent of all fractures in kids and teens. They occur twice as often in boys than in girls because girls are often done growing before they play the kinds of sports that put them at risk for growth plate injuries. Most growth plate injuries occur in boys between the ages of 14 and 16 and girls between the ages of 11 and 13.

Growth plate injuries to the foot or ankle can occur during contact sports—for example, after a fall or blow during a football game—or from chronic overuse, such as in the case of a gymnast who practices for hours on end or a long-distance runner who steps up his or her mileage. The sports that are most likely to lead to growth plate injuries include football, basketball, track and field, and gymnastics.

Symptoms of a growth plate injury include pain that interferes with athletic performance, decreased range of motion in the affected area, and the inability to put pressure on your foot or ankle.

If you experience any of the above symptoms, see your doctor. Left untreated, a growth plate injury may cause permanent damage and interfere with your growth. To diagnose a growth plate injury, your doctor will perform a physical examination and order an X-ray, CT scan, or MRI to take a closer look at the affected area.

For the best care, you may want to see an orthopedic surgeon who specializes in bone and joint problems in children and adolescents. Treatment will involve immobilization with a splint, cast, and/or crutches. If the growth plate is displaced, the doctor will need to put the bones back into place using either his or her hands (called manipulation) or by performing surgery. Following surgery, a cast will help keep the bones immobilized.

After the injury has healed, strengthening and range-of-motion exercises will help you return to everyday activities. Most growth plate injuries, especially those that occur in the foot or ankle, heal without any lasting problems. The time required to heal before returning to play varies depending on the individual and the type of injury, but it usually takes several weeks.

STRETCHING AND STRENGTHENING EXERCISES FOR THE FOOT AND ANKLE

Alphabet range-of-motion exercise. Sit in a chair and cross your affected leg over your other leg at your knee. Using your big toe as a

What is Sever's Disease?

Sever's disease is a growth plate injury of the heel. The foot is one of the first body parts to grow to its full size, which usually occurs during early puberty. At this time, the bones in the foot grow faster than the tendons and muscles, which makes the tendons and muscles tight and the heel less flexible. Any sport that requires activity performed while standing may put too much pressure on the back of the heel where the Achilles tendon attaches. This pressure can cause an injury in the heel and lead to Sever's disease.

Children and teenagers are most at risk for Sever's disease in the early part of their growth spurt—between ages eight and 10 for girls and 10 and 12 for boys. For this reason, the disease rarely strikes teens after age 15.

Symptoms of Sever's disease include heel pain in one or both heels, which usually starts after a child or teenager begins a new sports season. To diagnose Sever's disease, a doctor may use what's called the "squeeze test," where he or she squeezes both sides of the heel toward the back; if this is painful, Sever's disease is likely.

Treatment for Sever's disease includes stopping any activity that causes pain and icing the area for 20 minutes at a time, three times a day. A doctor may also prescribe orthotics to help keep the arches supported. Exercises to stretch the hamstrings and calf muscles may also help.

Much like the analogous *Osgood Schlatter syndrome* in the knee, with proper treatment, most athletes can return to play following a diagnosis of Sever's disease in about two to eight weeks, as soon as the heel pain disappears.

pointer, trace the capital letters of the alphabet from A to Z in the air. Hold your big toe rigid so all of the motion comes from your ankle. Repeat every hour that you are awake. The letters will get bigger as your range of motion improves.

One-legged stance with eyes closed. Stand in front of a mirror barefoot or on a pillow, cushion, or ankle disc. Bend your left leg at the knee so it is behind you and parallel with the floor and you are standing on your right leg only. As you draw your left leg off the floor, tighten your right buttock and transfer your weight to your right leg. Return your leg to the floor and switch sides, repeating three to five times on each side.

Ankle turn. Sit on a counter so your legs dangle. Take a long rope and put it under the arch of the shoe of your affected foot and hold the ends of the rope at knee height. Turn your ankle as far as it will go to the inside. Then pull the inside part of the rope and force your ankle to the outside, working against the resistance of the rope. When your foot is all the way out, pull on the outside of the rope as you bring your foot back to the inside, working against the resistance. Repeat until your ankle is fatigued.

Foot lift (outward). Sit on a counter and hang a weight on your toes. Point your foot up and turn your ankle as far as it will go to the outside. Repeat as many times as you can. Start with a five-pound weight and work your way up to heavier weights.

Foot lift (inward). Sitting on a counter, hang a weight on your toes, point your foot up, and turn your ankle as far as it will go toward the inside. Repeat as many times as you can. Start with a five-pound weight and work your way up to heavier weights.

Outer calf (gastrocnemius) stretch. Sit with both legs straight out in front of you. Loop a rope or towel around the ball of one of your feet, flex your foot back toward your ankle with your toes toward your knee. Hold for 10 seconds, then switch sides.

Inner calf (soleus) stretch. Sit with one leg straight and one leg bent (you will be stretching the bent leg). Grasp the bottom of the foot of your bent leg, and keeping your heel on the ground, pull your foot toward your body as far as it will go. Hold for 10 seconds, then switch sides.

Heel cord (Achilles tendon) stretch. Place the leg to be stretched in front of you with your toes raised up on a step or other elevation. Bend the knee and lean forward to make it bend more. Hold for between 10 and 30 seconds and repeat three times.

WHAT YOU NEED TO KNOW

> There are two main types of ankle injuries—sprains and fractures. Although they are very different injuries, both sprains

and fractures cause swelling and bruising. An ankle with only minimal swelling may be broken, while one with significant swelling may only be sprained. For this reason, you should seek medical attention—including an X-ray—for any injury to your ankle, especially if you feel pain on the inside of the joint. In the meantime, treat your ankle with RICE to eliminate internal bleeding and swelling.

➤ The intense pain of a sprained ankle eases rather quickly, so you may be tempted to get back in the game, but you should resist this temptation unless you are evaluated and cleared to return.

➤ A growing teen who experiences a fall or blow during sports play may be more likely to injure a growth plate than to suffer a sprain.

➤ If you experience any symptoms of a growth plate injury, see your doctor. Left untreated, a growth plate injury may cause permanent damage and interfere with your growth.

11

Non-Musculoskeletal Sports Injuries and Medical Conditions That May Restrict You

A few minutes after his high school tennis coach required the team to run two miles at a six-minute pace in the cold March weather, Cliff, 16, was huddled in his car, gasping for warmer air. After weeks of suffering from this each day, Cliff finally made an appointment to see his doctor and discovered he had exercise-induced asthma. The treatment: no running until the weather got warmer. At first, Cliff was fearful that his tennis career would be affected. But now, years later, Cliff has many years of competitive tennis under his belt, as well as a medical degree—in fact, he's the author of this book! Cliff knows as well as anyone that although certain medical conditions may make sports participation slightly more challenging for some teens, they can be successfully managed. Not all sports injuries fit into the categories of muscle, ligaments, and bone. In many cases, the injury involves something like a knocked-out tooth or a twisted testicle. Or the issue may be a temporary or permanent medical condition that places restrictions on certain sports such as exercise-induced asthma, a kidney infection, or *ringworm*. This chapter will cover non-musculoskeletal sports injuries and medical conditions that may place restrictions on certain activities and provide tips on what to do to best deal with both.

EXERCISE-INDUCED ASTHMA/ EXERCISE-INDUCED BRONCHOSPASM

The term *exercise-induced asthma,* (also known as "exercise-induced bronchospasm") is a condition that involves difficulty breathing associated with exercise. Symptoms, which usually last for several minutes, may be very vague; therefore, the condition often goes unrecognized. It is also underreported due to issues such as denial because of peer pressure, embarrassment, or fear of losing one's position on the team.

Exercise-induced asthma affects between seven and 20 percent of the population, and up to 80 percent of people who have asthma also suffer from exercise-induced asthmatic episodes.

If you suffer from exercise-induced asthma, you will be more likely to experience an attack if you exercise in air that is cool and dry, especially if you are exercising vigorously. Symptoms of exercise-induced asthma include a feeling of tightness in your chest, coughing, chest pain, trouble breathing, wheezing, and extreme tiredness that sets in around three minutes into activity. If you experience any of these symptoms while exercising, stop and rest immediately. Symptoms usually peak at about 15 minutes and resolve by 60 minutes.

If you have experienced an asthma attack while exercising and you suspect exercise-induced asthma, see your doctor. He or she will perform a test in which you walk on a treadmill for six to eight minutes in order to raise your heart rate to 85 percent of its maximum and then check the air capacity of your lungs (called spirometry). If you have never experienced an asthma attack before, your doctor may also test you for other possible causes of the episode, including gastroesophageal reflux disorder (GERD), *exercise-induced anaphylaxis,* or vocal cord dysfunction.

Luckily, you do not have to hang up your running shoes or soccer cleats if you are diagnosed with exercise-induced asthma. In fact, there are numerous athletes with exercise-induced asthma who have won Olympic metals and played professional sports. There are things you can do to prevent episodes from occurring, such as taking medications prescribed by your doctor, improving your cardiovascular fitness to decrease the stress on your lungs when you exercise, avoiding exercise in cold, dry air (or breathing through a loosely fitting scarf or mask when exercising in the cold), and using an inhaler when you start to feel symptoms.

You should also be aware of a phenomenon called the "refractory phase," a period of relative protection from the troubling symptoms of exercise-induced asthma that typically starts less than one hour after initial aerobic exercise and lasts up to three hours. During this period, the degree of bronchospasm (narrowing of the airways) is about one-half of the first episode. In certain cases, athletes can take advantage of this refractory phase, usually by exercising in several two- to three-minute increments as "warm-ups" 10 to 20 minutes before the main physical activity. This may induce a period of up to one hour during which exercise-induced asthma does not develop. This precaution

When an Illness Should Keep You on the Sidelines

It's an age-old dilemma among athletes: Should you exercise with a cold? An upper respiratory infection? The flu? Sometimes getting out there can help you feel better when you have a nagging cold. But if it's something more severe like the flu, not only could it make you feel much worse in the short term, it could prolong the illness. Here are some general guidelines to follow:

- ▶ If your symptoms are above the neck and you have no fever, it is probably safe to exercise. You shouldn't exercise vigorously, however, until your symptoms have been gone for a few days.

- ▶ If you have exercise-induced asthma, refrain from exercising if you have any type of respiratory issue, be it a cold, an upper respiratory infection, or the flu, as these illnesses can worsen the condition.

- ▶ If you are getting over a cold and still feel a little under the weather, you can participate in sports if the activity doesn't make you feel worse and you do not have a fever.

- ▶ If you have a fever as a result of any condition, refrain from all activity until your temperature returns to normal.

- ▶ If you have any symptoms of the flu—fever, extreme tiredness, aches, or swollen lymph nodes—refrain from exercising for at least two weeks.

mostly benefits those whose duration of planned activity is short, such as sprinters.

There are also some preliminary studies showing benefits of diets rich in omega-3 fatty acids in people with exercise-induced asthma. You can boost your intake of omega-3s by eating fatty fish two to three times a week, taking fish oil capsules, or eating more foods supplemented with fish oil, such as milk and peanut butter (there are more and more of these foods these days).

EXERCISE-INDUCED ANAPHYLAXIS

Along the same lines as exercise-induced asthma, but potentially much more severe, is exercise-induced anaphylaxis. With this syndrome, athletes experience symptoms of anaphylaxis—a severe whole-body allergic reaction—after increased physical activity. These symptoms include fatigue, warmth, hives, trouble breathing, nausea, vomiting, and in severe cases, extremely low high blood pressure that can be life-threatening.

Many sports can lead to exercise-induced anaphylaxis, including tennis, swimming, running, basketball, and others. Exercise-induced anaphylaxis seems to be worse in extremely hot or cold weather, as well as after an athlete has been exposed to a food allergen. A physician with experience treating exercise-induced anaphylaxis may be able to identify triggers so that you can probably resume normal activity with minimal danger of future episodes.

If you or a teammate experiences symptoms of exercise-induced anaphylaxis during sports practice or competition, call 911 immediately. Exercise-induced anaphylaxis is a life-threatening condition that has led to a few deaths in high school athletes, so emergency treatment is critical.

MONONUCLEOSIS (MONO)

Often called the "kissing disease," infectious mononucleosis (mono) is a virus transmitted through saliva. In addition to kissing, mono can be transmitted by sharing a glass or utensils with an infected person, sneezing, or coughing.

Mono strikes teenagers more than any other age group and causes symptoms such as extreme tiredness and weakness, sore throat or a strep throat that doesn't respond to antibiotics, fever, swollen lymph nodes in the neck and armpits, swollen tonsils, headache, skin rash, loss of appetite, night sweats, and an enlarged spleen that may be vulnerable to rupture, especially if subjected to trauma. Mono also strikes children and adults, but it is less likely to lead to as many symptoms in these age groups.

The two symptoms of mono most important to watch out for in teenagers who play competitive sports are fatigue and spleen enlargement. More than half of teenagers with mono experience an enlarged spleen within the first two weeks of infection; these teens should avoid any activity that could lead to a spleen rupture. The extreme fatigue associated with mono often makes playing sports extremely difficult. As a rule, all athletes with mono should avoid playing contact sports (football, rugby, hockey, gymnastics, wrestling, diving, basketball, or lacrosse) for at least four weeks after first experiencing symptoms. If you participate in a noncontact sport such as running, you may be able to get back on the track or course sooner if your doctor gives you the green light. If there is any question as to whether or not your spleen is still enlarged, your doctor may choose to conduct an ultrasound to make sure it is safe for you to return to all activities.

TESTICULAR TORSION (TWISTED TESTICLE)

A testicular torsion is a condition that results from a twisting of one or both of the testicles during sports play, other activity, or in some cases, sleep. When the testicle twists, it strangles the spermatic cord, cutting off blood supply to the testicle. Twisted testicles are particularly common in teen boys between the ages of 12 and 18, but they can occur at any age. If one or both of your testicles have not descended into your scrotum (a conditioned called cryptochidism), you are at a higher risk for a twisted testicle. If it goes untreated, a twisted testicle can lead to shrinkage or tissue death in the testicle, and in severe cases may require that the testicle be surgically removed.

Symptoms of a testicular torsion include sudden, severe testicle pain that begins to subside after a few hours (when tissue death sets in), lower abdominal pain, blood in semen, a lump in the testicle, nausea and vomiting, and redness and swelling of the testicle.

A twisted testicle is a medical emergency, so if you suspect you've suffered one, seek medical attention right away. Your physician will perform a physical examination and ask you about your symptoms. If he or she has any doubt about whether or not you indeed have a testicular torsion, he or she may order an ultrasound, perform a urinalysis to rule out a bacterial infection, or in rare cases, order a surgical exploration.

Treatment for a testicular torsion involves untwisting the testicle (called detorsion), either manually or surgically. If there is any tissue death, the dead tissue will need to be removed with surgery, possibly along with the testicle if the case is severe. If the torsion is diagnosed and treated within five to six hours of when it occurred, you will probably suffer no complications. If 18 to 24 hours go by, you will be at increased risk for tissue death and, therefore, losing the testicle. Ice/cold packs often help to reduce the pain and inflammation. If you have surgery, you might be given a scrotal support to wear for about a week. You will be able to return to play once you can tolerate the activity without pain. You should build up to your original level of activity gradually.

ATHLETES MISSING PAIRED ORGANS

If you are missing a paired organ (i.e., kidney, eye, testicle) and are considering participation in a sport, you will need to consider the risks of severe injury to your remaining organ and discuss this with your doctor, your parents, and your coach. This is a difficult decision, and there often isn't a clear answer. The best thing you can do is educate yourself on the risks of the sport to the remaining organ, weighed against how important it is to you to participate in the sport.

RINGWORM

Ringworm is actually not a worm at all—it's a fungal skin infection that lives on the dead tissues of the skin, hair, and nails. Ringworm is so named because of the ring pattern the resulting rash makes on the skin.

In most cases, teenage athletes catch ringworm from other players and teammates—either person-to-person during contact sports (especially wrestling, gymnastics, or other sports that require mats) or from the locker room.

Symptoms of ringworm include a round or oval rash with a raised border that starts small and slowly grows larger. As the rash spreads, the center part of the oval becomes clear. There may also be itching, scaly skin, and small pus-filled bumps as part of the infection. If the rash strikes the scalp, it can causes patches of hair loss.

If you suspect ringworm, see your doctor. He or she will prescribe a cream or an oral medicine to kill the fungus causing the rash. Because it is so contagious, ringworm often infects an entire team and returns after treatment. If you've been infected with ringworm, you will likely be held from participation in any sports that require skin contact (especially wrestling). Here are a few helpful tips on how to keep the infection at bay:

> ➤ Try to keep your skin dry; fungus is more likely to grow on moist skin.

> Use the medicine you've been prescribed according to label directions. If the medication is in the form of a cream, rub it into your skin well and do not use excessive amounts.
> If you have a ringworm infection on your scalp, shampoo your hair every day with the shampoo prescribed by your doctor.

To help prevent infection in the first place, do the following:

> Wash any clothes, towels, or bedding that may have come into contact with someone with ringworm.
> If you participate in gymnastics, wrestling, or martial arts, request that the mats be cleaned regularly.
> If you or someone else on your team has a rash, do not share clothes or personal care items and make sure that they and/or the coach is aware.

HERPES GLADIATORUM

Herpes gladiatorum—similar to oral herpes and also typically caused by HSV-1—can be passed around during high school contact sports, particularly wrestling. In fact, it is one of the most common infections that occur as a result of sports contact.

HSV-1 is a viral infection that spreads through skin-to-skin contact. It begins as a group of small red sores around the mouth that blister and then disappear in about two weeks. Once you've been infected with the virus, it stays in your body forever, and it can erupt at any time. An estimated nine out of 10 people carry the herpes virus, many of whom don't even know it.

During competitions, wrestlers have a lot of contact with their opponents' heads and necks, which is why the herpes virus spreads so easily; skin contact is the primary mode of transmission. In addition, studies show that the virus can spread via mats and other equipment.

To help prevent the spread of the HSV-1 during competitions, athletes who participate in contact sports who have the virus should refrain from competing when they are having an outbreak. They should also consider an antiviral medication such as acyclovir (Zovirax) under the direction of their doctors.

IMPETIGO

One of the most common skin infections in kids, impetigo is a contagious condition that produces blisters or sores on the neck, hands, face, or groin. Although impetigo most frequently infects preschool and school-age kids, it can also strike high school athletes, particularly wrestlers or others who play contact sports.

What to Do with a Knocked-out Tooth

If you play a contact sport such as football, basketball, or rugby, chances are you have—or you know someone who has—knocked out a tooth. If you suffer an injury to your face or mouth and find yourself without one or more teeth as a result, you should seek emergency medical care right away. But in the meantime, there are some things you can do that may make the difference between saving your tooth and having to get a fake one. Here are some tips:

▶ If the tooth has been completely knocked out, you may gently clean it off, but do not scrub it. Hold the tooth by the crown (top) instead of the root to avoid damaging the ligaments.

▶ If you can stand it, place the tooth gently in its socket as you ride to the hospital. If you find this too uncomfortable, transport the tooth to the doctor in saliva, saline, or milk—not in water. As an alternative, you may also place the tooth back in your mouth, between your cheek and your gum line.

▶ Whatever you do, do not transport the tooth dry—this will cause damage within minutes. Transporting it in water can be equally as damaging.

▶ If you are bleeding from the socket, rinse your mouth out with water, place a wad of tissue or some gauze in the socket, and bite down on it—the pressure should stop the bleeding.

▶ If you have a loose, broken, or pushed-in tooth, avoid eating or drinking anything until you get medical attention.

▶ If the tooth is broken in pieces, retrieve any remaining parts and transport them in saline, saliva, or milk.

In high school athletes, impetigo can spread by way of skin-to-skin contact during wrestling, basketball, football, and other sports. It can also spread through locker rooms on clothing or towels that have touched infected skin.

Symptoms of impetigo include itchy blisters that may or may not have a crusted appearance on the face, hands, neck, or groin. If you experience any of these symptoms, see your doctor as soon as possible—he or she will prescribe an antibiotic cream or pill to help wipe out the infection. In the meantime, refrain from playing your sport until the blisters have completely disappeared.

To prevent an impetigo infection, wash your hands regularly and take showers after all sports competition, particularly if you play a sport that puts you in direct contact with other athletes' skin.

MEDICAL CONDITIONS THAT CAN BE DANGEROUS WHEN MIXED WITH SPORTS

Teens with medical conditions present special challenges when it comes to participation in sports. If you have a medical condition that could be dangerous if mixed with athletic performance, look to your family doctor or pediatrician to help guide you on how to exercise safely and refrain from participating in any new activity without clearance from your doctor. Here is a list of conditions that may be dangerous when mixed with sports:

> ➤ Bleeding disorders
> ➤ Cardiovascular disease (including congenital heart disease and heart murmurs)
> ➤ Diabetes
> ➤ Infectious diarrhea
> ➤ Eating disorders
> ➤ Fever
> ➤ History of heat illness
> ➤ HIV infection
> ➤ Hepatitis
> ➤ Seizure disorder
> ➤ Obesity
> ➤ Pregnancy
> ➤ Respiratory conditions such as asthma or respiratory infection
> ➤ Lupus
> ➤ Sickle-cell disease
> ➤ Enlarged spleen
> ➤ Testicle problems (enlarged testicle or undescended testicle)

TRANSMISSIBLE DISEASES AND CONTACT SPORTS

If you play a sport—particularly if you play a contact sport such as football, wrestling, or rugby—you are at an increased risk for contracting an infectious disease. Not only do athletes come into contact with one another during sports practice and competition, they also travel together and share space in the locker room—all of which make infection with a transmissible disease much more likely.

Some of the most common infectious diseases in teen athletes include herpes simplex infections, ringworm, measles, and bacterial skin infections such as impetigo. More dangerous infectious diseases such as hepatitis, HIV, meningitis, and methicillin-resistant S aureus (MRSA) have caused some concern as well.

Infectious diseases travel in a few different ways from athlete to athlete—from direct contact such as skin-on-skin contact between wrestlers, through indirect contact by way of respiration, blood, or fecal-oral exposure, or through sharing equipment, clothing, water coolers, or towels.

To decrease your chances of acquiring an infectious disease through sports play, here are a few things you can do:

➤ To avoid ringworm and other skin infections, do not share clothing or athletic equipment.
➤ Do not share bars of soap with teammates.
➤ Make sure you are up-to-date on all your immunizations.
➤ Wash your hands and use hand sanitizer regularly.
➤ Make sure all shared sports equipment is properly disinfected.

WHAT YOU NEED TO KNOW

➤ Symptoms of exercise-induced asthma include a feeling of tightness in your chest, coughing, chest pain, trouble breathing, wheezing, and extreme tiredness that sets in around three minutes into activity. If you experience any of these symptoms while exercising, stop and rest immediately. Symptoms usually peak at about 15 minutes and resolve by 60 minutes.
➤ If you or a teammate experience symptoms of exercise-induced anaphylaxis (which include extreme fatigue, warmth, hives, and trouble breathing) during sports practice or competition, call 911 immediately. EIA is a life-threatening condition that has led to a few deaths in high school athletes.

➤ As a rule, all athletes with mono should avoid playing contact sports (football, rugby, hockey, gymnastics, wrestling, diving, basketball, or lacrosse) for at least four weeks after first experiencing symptoms. If you participate in a noncontact sport such as running, you may be able to get back on the track or course sooner if your doctor gives you the green light.

➤ A twisted testicle is a medical emergency, so if you suspect you've suffered one, seek medical attention right away. If it goes untreated, a twisted testicle can lead to shrinkage or tissue death in the testicle, and in severe cases, may require surgical removal of the testicle.

12

Sports-Specific Injuries

We've all heard the phrase, "An ounce of prevention is worth a pound of cure," and this holds especially true for sports injuries. All sports have different athletic requirements, and so they carry different injury risks. Both acute and chronic/overuse injuries can often be prevented or minimized by proper preparation, including physical fitness (strength, flexibility, agility, etc.) directed at the specific sport, appropriate gear (protective equipment, or proper fitting/type of gear), the right technique, and appropriate levels of participation and training in the sport.

This chapter will review some of the biomechanics and activities involved in popular sports, as well as some of the more common acute and chronic/overuse injuries associated with these sports and how you can dramatically reduce your risk of sustaining one of these injuries. Since there are too many sports to cover in this chapter, you may need to look for the activity that most closely resembles your sport in its mechanics. Also, keep in mind that not all injuries associated with a given sport will be mentioned—only the ones that are particularly common in that sport. For more detail about a particular injury, refer back to that injury in one of the previous chapters.

RUNNING

Running is associated with multiple injuries, most of which involve the lower extremity. A majority of these are overuse injuries, which often result from long-distance running. Proper mechanics throughout the entire lower-extremity kinetic chain, from the back to the feet, go a long way in preventing running injuries, as do strength and flexibility exercises. If you have an overuse injury in your lower extremity, you should always be screened for biomechanical issues, including areas of relative weakness and asymmetries like leg-length differences. Occasionally, orthotics or inserts can correct these imbalances or asymmetries. If you are a long-distance runner, you should be careful to increase your mileage slowly and gradually to avoid injury, following the guidelines of your training protocol or doctor (usually 10 percent increases per week).

Hip abduction strengthening (with side-to-side shuffling, sometimes with a band providing resistance), hamstring stretching, iliotibial band stretching (stretching the outer thigh), quadriceps strengthening (squats, lunges, leg raises, wall sits at a 30-degree angle and up), and ankle stability exercises (standing on one foot, with eyes closed if possible, or using ankle discs) can all help maximize your running biomechanics.

Hip injuries, including hip flexor strains and hamstring strains, are also frequently seen in runners. To help prevent these injuries, it is important to maintain flexibility and strength in your hip flexors/iliopsoas, hamstring, calf muscles and Achilles tendons.

Patellofemoral syndrome (runner's knee) is a common knee injury in runners. In addition to the rehabilitative exercises mentioned above, a patellofemoral brace may help keep your kneecap properly aligned and can be an excellent aid to keep you running while you are undergoing rehabilitation. If you have problems stemming from your feet such as overpronation, you may benefit from orthotics or athletic inserts.

Patellar tendonitis is a repetitive strain of the patellar tendon—the tendon that allows the quadriceps muscle to straighten the knee. The exercises mentioned above are often helpful in reducing strain to this tendon. A patellar tendon strap, positioned tightly below the kneecap, may also help to provide support, especially while the injury is healing.

Iliotibial band (ITB) syndrome is a common knee injury that often affects long-distance runners when they reach a certain distance. In addition to the above exercises, an ITB strap can help you keep running while the injury is healing.

Shin splints/medial tibial stress syndrome is very common in runners, especially distance runners. The injury often results from biomechanical problems, rapid increases in training, and incorrect footwear. If you are having pain during or after running, you should be evaluated by a physician to rule out a stress fracture or *chronic exertional compartment syndrome* and to find out the cause so it can be corrected. In most cases, athletes can resume running once the injury has been properly rested and rehabilitated. If you are a female and are missing your periods, or you have a history of eating disorders or stress fractures, you should inform your physician because you are at higher risk for a stress fracture.

FOOTBALL

Few sports involve as many high-impact collisions as football. Players frequently experience concussions, as well as neck and shoulder injuries, usually as a result of open field tackling. One of the best ways to avoid these injuries is to refrain from any form of spear tackling—an open field tackle executed with your head flexed forward—at all costs. Spear tackling puts you at high risk of potentially devastating injuries that could result in paralysis or death. If you or another player appears to have sustained a significant head or neck injury, you should not be touched or moved until a highly trained professional can make sure there isn't a severe injury to the neck. Even the slightest movement to an acutely injured neck can result in paralysis or even death.

Burners/stingers occur often in football as a result of a traction force through the shoulder and neck, which causes the nerves to stretch and results in transient numbness in the arm. (If you experience arm numbness, seek medical treatment immediately.) Once your symptoms are gone and your arms are strong, you may be allowed to return to play with the permission of your doctor.

Upper extremity injuries are also commonly seen in football. Protective gear does help prevent these injuries, but shoulder dislocations, AC joint sprains, elbow and wrist fractures, and other injuries to the upper extremity still do occur. A common football injury to the hand is a jersey finger, which is a ruptured flexor tendon in the finger that typically results from grabbing onto another player's jersey that then gets forcefully jerked away. A jersey finger requires prompt surgical repair, as any delay in diagnosis or treatment can result in permanent disability. Another common hand injury is skiers/gamekeeper's thumb, which occurs when the thumb is bent away from the hand, injuring the ulnar collateral ligament. In some cases, skier's thumb requires surgery, and the injury always requires splinting. Finger injuries are common in teen athletes, and some can be treated with splinting or even buddy taping (taping it to an adjacent finger). Just to be safe, you should seek medical evaluation for any hand injury.

Football is also notorious for knee injuries, including ACL, MCL and meniscus injuries. Sometimes these injuries are unavoidable, depending on the specific circumstances. However, strengthening exercises for the hip and knee area can prevent knee injuries in many cases.

Ankle injuries occur frequently in football, often when one player steps on another player's foot. You can return to play following an ankle injury once you can perform running drills without pain. Initially, you may need to wear an ankle brace or tape the area. Unfortunately, once you experience an ankle injury, you are at risk for another one because the ankle is still weak and vulnerable. One way to minimize risk of a future injury is with aggressive exercises geared toward balance, range of motion, and strengthening.

ICE HOCKEY

Ice hockey can lead to a wide variety of both acute and chronic injuries. The movements involved with the sport stress various tissues in the body, and the collisions can result in injuries to almost any body part. That's why appropriate equipment and protective gear are so important. Here are some of the most common ice hockey–related injuries:

Contusions may result from being struck by the stick, the puck, another player, or from hitting the boards or ice. Contusions should be iced and evaluated as appropriate. If you're returning to the game, doughnut pads may provide protection from reinjury.

Groin pain is a common complaint in skaters; it may result from groin/adductor strains, hip flexor strains, sports hernias, pubic dysfunctions, and other injuries. These injuries will often get better with rest and physical therapy, though surgery is occasionally necessary (especially in cases of persistent sports hernias).

Knee injuries of virtually any type can occur in skaters, the most common being medial collateral ligament (MCL) injuries, due to the stress placed on the knee when the skate is planted. The risk for these and other knee injuries can be minimized by maintaining strength and flexibility in your lower extremity.

Shoulder injuries usually result from collisions and falls. Acromioclavicular (AC joint) sprains often occur during collisions with other players, the ice, or the boards. "Checking" also commonly leads to these types of injuries. Protective gear and avoidance of unnecessary risky maneuvers go far in the prevention of many hockey-related shoulder injuries.

Foot and ankle injuries that occur in hockey are often related to weakness in the ankles or even higher up in the knee or hip. Therefore, hockey-related foot and ankle injuries can usually be minimized with proper sports-specific strengthening in the lower extremity.

SOCCER

Soccer is a very physical sport that involves constant and repetitive running and sprinting, as well as twisting, turning, sliding, and other movements that require a great deal of athleticism. If you're not in good shape, you will find out very quickly when you play soccer. Because of the wide variety of movements the sport requires, virtually any body part is at risk for a range of injuries. Here are some of the most common:

Contusions are very common in soccer, and they usually result from a kick by or collision with another player or a fall to the ground. Contusions should be evaluated by a medical professional. In the meantime, you should use ice and compression to prevent swelling. When you are able to return to play, a doughnut pad may help to protect the area.

Upper extremity injuries (wrist and elbow fractures, shoulder injuries, etc.) often result from falling and should be evaluated immediately by a medical professional.

Knee injuries are extremely common in soccer; they include MCL and ACL injuries, meniscus tears, patellar subluxations and dislocations, and the overuse injuries patellofemoral syndrome, patellar tendonopathy, ITB syndrome, etc.

Finally, ankle and foot injuries can result from kicking, twisting, turning, stepping on other players' feet, etc., during soccer. As when they occur in other sports, foot and ankle injuries should be evaluated and treated by a physician or other individual with appropriate training. Strengthening exercises and taping/bracing can help prevent foot and ankle injuries from recurring.

WRESTLING

A sport that involves matching direct forces between the entire bodies of two opposing athletes, wrestling can be quite strenuous and can potentially cause injuries of virtually any type and in any body part. Strains, sprains, dislocations, and fractures are all common in wrestling. Some injuries and conditions, however, are somewhat unique to the sport, including the following:

Auricular hematoma/cauliflower ear is very common in wrestling, due to the grabbing and tugging nature of the sport, and it can be very problematic, especially from an aesthetic point of view. If you have a swollen or deformed ear, you should promptly see an ear, nose, and throat (ENT) specialist or primary care/sports medicine physician who is comfortable treating this injury. The doctor will likely use a needle to drain the fluid from your ear and then apply a compressive dressing or splint to prevent it from filling up with fluid again. If this is not done in a timely manner, the swelling can harden due to cartilage growth (*cauliflower ear*), leading to a deformity that is far more difficult to treat.

Nosebleeds (also called epistaxis) are often seen in wrestlers for similar reasons. Firm, uninterrupted compression (pinching the nostrils together), perhaps along with ice, will usually control the bleed. Topical Phenylephrine (an ingredient in nasal spray) applied to the inner nostril may further control the bleeding. Some team physicians will have silver nitrite or an electrocautery device on hand to cauterize the bleed.

Infections such as impetigo, tinea corporis (*ringworm*), and herpes gladiatorum are easily transmitted between wrestlers through skin-to-skin contact and mats. In most cases, athletes suspected of having these infections are disqualified from competition until they have resolved. To help prevent spreading, if you think you or another wrestler has one of these conditions, tell your coach or referee immediately. It is always a good idea to make sure that all mats are properly cleaned with an antiseptic.

GYMNASTICS

Gymnastics involves many different routines and requires use of virtually all muscle groups in the upper and lower extremities and trunk. If you participate in gymnastics, you should choose a physician and/or physical therapist who has good knowledge of and experience working with gymnasts. Ideally, this person should be in close communication with your coach. USA Gymnastics maintains a referral list of physicians and other health-care providers who have demonstrated specific experience and skill in working with gymnasts. Here are a few injuries common to gymnastics:

Back strains, spondylolysis, and spondylolisthesis are very common in gymnasts due to the continuous extension of the back. Tight hamstrings often contribute to these injuries and, therefore, should be addressed aggressively during rehabilitation. Strong core and back muscles and adequate flexibility (i.e., hamstrings, etc.) help to prevent back injuries. Unfortunately, some gymnasts are at increased risk simply because of the way they're built. If you are having pain in your back while arching or during/after any activity, or increased tightness in your hamstrings, you should stop all activity and see a doctor as soon as possible.

Wrist strains, including posterior capsule strains, are very common in gymnastics, as gymnasts often use their upper extremities in much the same way other athletes use the lower extremities. Gymnasts have even been known to get stress fractures in their forearms due to the repetitive strenuous demands of the sport. Proper strengthening and flexibility throughout the upper extremities—as well as in the core—is very important in preventing these injuries.

Ankle injuries (sprains, strains, and fractures) are a constant problem for many gymnasts, disrupting their training time and time again. A major reason for recurrent ankle injuries is that once you injure your ankle, the supporting muscles immediately weaken and are, therefore, unable to protect against repeated strain. If you have recently healed from an ankle injury (even if the injury occurred a long time ago), try this: Stand on your good foot, then carefully close your eyes and try to hold your stance. Repeat with the injured ankle. You will probably notice that you are far more shaky and unstable on the injured side—an indication that the ankle is still at significant increased risk of repeat injury and therefore needs to be strengthened.

BASKETBALL

Basketball involves many rapid athletic maneuvers on a very unforgiving hard surface, coupled with interference from other players; therefore, the sport poses a risk for many different injuries, both acute and overuse. The entire lower extremity is constantly challenged in basketball, making the area vulnerable to the following injuries:

Jumper's knee (patellar tendonopathy) results from frequent jumping and other strenuous maneuvers. Strengthening exercises and avoidance of aggravating movements are usually all that's necessary for treatment. A patellar tendon strap (if applied properly) can also be very helpful in protecting the damaged tendon from reinjury, so it may help to get you back in the game more quickly.

Patellofemoral syndrome is caused by similar factors and treated in much the same way. For more information on patellofemoral syndrome, see "runner's knee" above and look for the injury in the knee chapter. MCL, ACL, and meniscus injuries can also occur in basketball and need to be managed appropriately.

Ankle injuries occur all too frequently in basketball, often caused by landing on another player's foot after a jump. Lateral ankle sprains are the most common, and with each sprain, the ankle becomes weaker and more vulnerable to further injury.

Proprioceptive exercises (exercises that improve balance) should be done aggressively, once tolerated, as they help to strengthen the ankle and prevent it from rolling. Premature return to basketball after an ankle injury will place you at an even higher risk for reinjury. Taping and/or bracing, if done properly, can help to protect the injured ankle during this period, but it does not fully replace the protection provided by well-coordinated muscle strength.

Finger injuries often occur after fingers are jammed by the ball or twisted by another player's hand or fingers and occasionally result in fractures, ligament sprains, or tendon injuries. Since some finger injuries require immediate treatment, possibly even surgery, they should be evaluated as soon as possible by a physician or other trained professional. Many finger injuries (including some fractures) can be effectively treated by splinting or buddy taping. Once a finger injury has healed, range-of-motion injuries are important to keep the finger from stiffening.

VOLLEYBALL

Much like basketball, volleyball is played on an unforgiving hard surface (except in beach volleyball), so it puts athletes at risk for similar injuries in the lower extremity. Jumper's knee (patellar tendonopathy) frequently occurs due to the repetitive jumping requirements of the sport. Ankle injuries are also relatively common, especially when a player lands from a high jump (such as during a spike or a block) onto another player's foot. Again, plyometric training is an excellent way to minimize injury risk and improve performance in volleyball.

Shoulder injuries in volleyball typically occur during spiking and occasionally during blocking or setting. Rotator cuff and biceps tendonitis are very common, as is instability in the shoulder joint, which stretches the tissues around it. Flexibility exercises for the chest, thorax, and shoulder, as well as strengthening exercises for the core, scapular, and rotator cuff will dramatically reduce your risk of shoulder injuries and improve your performance in volleyball overall.

Finger injuries often occur from being jammed by the ball and occasionally result in fractures, ligament sprains, or tendon injuries. Treatment for these injuries is the same as treatment for finger injuries that result from basketball, described above.

BASEBALL/SOFTBALL

Pitching and throwing in both baseball and softball often cause injuries to the shoulder and elbow. Pitchers are at an increased risk, given the number of times they are required to throw in a game or training session.

Baseball pitching places a large amount of stress on the shoulder, causing instability (especially in the structures in the front of the shoulder) and injuries to the rotator cuff, labrum, biceps tendon, and other structures. The underhanded softball pitch places extreme stress on the biceps tendon as well as the other structures in the front of the shoulder. Some players have shoulders that can naturally handle these stresses, especially those who started pitching at a young age. Other players seem to have difficulty with pitching/throwing, no matter how hard they try; these athletes may need to cut back or stop pitching (and, in rare cases, stop throwing altogether).

Elbow injuries also commonly result from throwing, including Little League elbow, medial epicondylitis, ulnar collateral ligament (UCL) injuries, osteochondritis dessicans (OCD), and others. These injuries often improve with rest, though some (typically the UCL and OCD injuries) may require surgery.

Both shoulder and elbow injuries are best prevented by strengthening programs that maximize body mechanics during the throwing motion. Stretching the upper torso to allow proper rotation, core and scapular stabilization, and rotator cuff strengthening is also important. If you've been treated for one of these injuries and advised against pitching/throwing and these rehabilitative measures have not been addressed, ask your physician or consider getting another opinion.

TENNIS

When played competitively, tennis can be extremely rigorous, requiring a lot of coordinated strength, flexibility, quickness, and agility in both the upper and lower extremities. Additionally, some of the more recent developments in tennis gear (i.e., stiffer strings, etc.) place further strain on the body tissues of many players. Since much of your power comes from your hips and trunk, strength in these areas is crucial to minimizing injuries and increasing performance. Coordinated strength and flexibility from the trunk and upper extremity down through the core and lower extremity can offer protection against acute and overuse injuries in all these areas, not to mention improved performance.

Upper and lower back strains, upper extremity injuries (shoulder, elbow, wrist/hand), and lower extremity injuries (knee and ankle strains and sprains) are also all too common in tennis players. Here are a few of the more well known injuries:

Tennis elbow (lateral epicondylitis) is mostly seen in novice tennis players and typically results from using poor mechanics (i.e., hitting backhands too late, which places strain on the wrist extensors). If you have tennis elbow, you're likely using an improper technique, so you should consider having a qualified tennis professional or coach look at your form. Also, tightness in trunk rotation or weakness in your shoulder/scapula can place your elbow at a mechanical disadvantage, so addressing these areas is every bit as important as addressing the elbow itself. In the meantime, you might get some relief and support from a properly fitted and placed tennis elbow strap.

Medial epicondylitis is often seen in more advanced tennis players and results from snapping of the wrist. Similarly, while the wrist snap may be very important for topspin and power, much of this force should be coming from the trunk and hips. Trunk and hip rotation stretches and strengthening can do wonders for your power and topspin while sparing the wrist from excessive strain. Again, scapular exercises are very important for prevention and treatment. Little League elbow may result from similar mechanical issues, so the same will hold true for this condition as well.

As for the shoulder, rotator cuff and biceps tendon strain, as well as anterior shoulder instability are rather common in tennis players, mostly due to the service motion. Again, adequate trunk rotation, as well as strength in the back, scapula, and core is crucial for sparing the shoulder from strain during these repetitive motions. If you notice the power of your serve fading or that your shoulder starts to hurt after several serves, you may have weakness in your scapula stabilizer muscles, and strengthening these muscles might not only protect the shoulder from injury but also help to improve and maintain the power and accuracy of your serves.

WHAT YOU NEED TO KNOW

> Both acute and chronic/overuse injuries can be prevented or minimized by proper preparation, including physical fitness (strength, flexibility, agility, etc.) directed at the specific sport, appropriate gear (protective equipment, or proper fitting/type of gear), the right technique, and appropriate levels of participation and training in the sport.

> If you are a runner, hip abduction strengthening (side-to-side shuffling is good, sometimes with a band providing resistance holding your feet together), hamstring stretching, iliotibial band stretching (stretching the outer thigh), quadriceps strengthening (squats, lunges, leg raises, wall sits at a 30-degree angle

and up), and ankle stability exercises (standing on one foot, with eyes closed if possible, or using ankle discs) can all help maximize your biomechanics and help to prevent injuries.

➤ If you play football, one effective way to minimize risk of a future injury is with aggressive exercises geared toward balance, range of motion, and strengthening.

➤ Appropriate equipment and protective gear are very important in contact sports such as football and ice hockey.

➤ Strengthening exercises and taping/bracing can help to prevent foot and ankle injuries from recurring in athletes who play soccer.

➤ USA Gymnastics maintains a referral list of physicians and other health-care providers who have demonstrated specific experience and skill in working with gymnasts.

➤ If you are having pain in your back while arching or during/after any activity, or increased tightness in your hamstrings, you should stop all activity and see a doctor as soon as possible.

13

Helping Friends and Family Cope with Sports Injuries

Casey, 15, has been practicing gymnastics since she learned to walk. Her best friend Ashley, also 15 and also a gymnast, has been at her side the entire time—they started together as toddlers, and they are both at the same competitive level on their high school team. As kids, they both dreamed of being on the Olympic gymnastics team someday. Unfortunately, Ashley's dreams were recently shattered after she suffered a devastating fall off the balance beam. The injury to her ankle will take her out for the rest of the season and perhaps out of gymnastics for the rest of her life. Ashley is sad, depressed, and frustrated, and Casey—who is doing better than ever in the sport—is not sure how to handle the situation.

Even if you've never suffered from a sports injury yourself, if a friend or family member is currently dealing with one, like Casey, you will be affected. If this friend or loved one approaches you for advice on how to deal with an injury and how to stay sane while resting, surely you will want to be prepared with the most helpful and appropriate things to do. This chapter will help you to know what to expect and how to help.

DEALING WITH A SPORTS INJURY DIAGNOSIS

An injury can be hard for anyone to face, but it can be particularly difficult for teenagers who play sports. As a supportive friend or family member of a teenager newly diagnosed with an injury, you can provide help and comfort.

First, if your friend or loved one has suffered a sports injury that is not healing on its own and he or she is resistant to seek treatment or rest, encourage the person to go to the doctor. After all, the only way to get proper treatment is by knowing for sure.

Next, understand that your friend or family member will likely go through a range of emotions following a sports injury diagnosis. Those feelings may be particularly strong for teens who suffer an injury that could take them out of their sports for the season, or worse, indefinitely. Understanding the specific emotions that go along with a sports injury diagnosis can help you to recognize where your friend or loved one is in the coping process.

Anger. When your friend or loved one is first sidelined by an injury, he or she is likely to feel angry at the unfairness of the situation. This anger may be especially strong if the person feels blameless for the injury (if it results from a particularly hard tackle on the football field or an illegal hold in wrestling, for example).

A *sense of lost identity*. If your friend or loved one eats, sleeps, and breathes the sport, he or she may feel very lost about taking a break from it. You can help the athlete by focusing on other things he or she excels in and encouraging the athlete to focus on those activities as well.

Fear and anxiety. Fear and anxiety are common reactions to sports injuries in teens, both in the athletes who suffer them and the teammates who serve as witnesses. The athlete will be fearful about the pain of the injury, how long it will keep her or him out of the sport, and how fellow teammates will treat the athlete while recovering. Teammates may see the injury as a reminder of their own vulnerability, and they may fear a similar fate.

Lost confidence. As fear and anxiety set in, the injured athlete may feel a sense of lost confidence, both in the ability to play the sport and to do other things. That's why it's important to bolster self-esteem by complimenting the athlete on other activities and giving encouragement to focus energy on those things for the time being.

Depression. Once the athlete accepts an injury as reality, he or she is likely to become depressed at the notion of having to take a break from the sport. Symptoms of depression include loss of interest in activities once loved, weight loss or gain, restlessness, or mental or physical fatigue. If you have noticed these symptoms in your friend or loved one, urge the athlete to talk to a health-care professional about feelings and talk to a parent or counselor right away; if left untreated, depression can lead to suicide.

HOW YOU CAN HELP A LOVED ONE COPE WITH A SPORTS INJURY

To best support your friend or loved one and help him or her through the sports injury—whether the recovery process lasts for two months or two years—here are some additional things you can do:

Listen. One of the best things you can do to offer support to your friend or loved one is to offer an ear. If he or she is feeling really down about the injury and needs to "vent," let the athlete do. Often people who suffer sports injuries or other setbacks don't need advice; they just need to get their feelings out by talking.

Watch. Sometimes teens who are used to spending most of their time on the soccer field or basketball court will use the newly acquired free time in the wrong ways—for example, to drink alcohol, do drugs, or commit crimes. The combination of free time and pent-up aggression from having to rest can be a bad combination. Watch for signs of troublesome behavior in your friend or loved one, and talk to a parent or school counselor if you start to notice a problem.

In addition, as mentioned above, watch out for signs of depression in your friend or loved one, such as loss of interest in activities once loved, weight loss or gain, restlessness, or mental or physical fatigue. If left untreated, this depression can lead to suicide, so urge him or her to talk to a health-care professional about feelings and talk to a parent or counselor right away.

Be there. One of the best ways for teens to avoid becoming depressed or turning to drugs, alcohol, or other troublesome behaviors following an injury is to spend time with friends in positive social situations. So urge your friend to join you at the movies, the mall (if walking isn't an issue), to get some ice cream, or to participate in other activities that will help to get his or her mind off the injury. If there are certain physical activities that your friend or loved one is permitted to engage in—such as biking—offer to do those things with him or her.

Don't project. If you also play a sport, particularly if you play the same sport as your friend or loved one who got hurt, an injury may serve as a reality check for you and make you feel vulnerable to injury yourself. Try to put those feelings aside for the sake of the other person. The last thing an injured athlete needs is to feel alienated by friends or teammates.

Overall, keep in mind that teenagers who have recently been diagnosed with a sports injury need the love and encouragement of their friends and family members more than ever. Whether it's your best friend, brother, sister, or cousin who is injured, your comfort and support will help ease both the physical and emotional burden.

WHAT YOU NEED TO KNOW

- Even if you have never suffered from a sports injury yourself, once a friend or family member is currently dealing with one, you, too, will be affected.
- As a supportive friend or family member of a teenager newly diagnosed with a sports injury, you can provide help and comfort.
- If your friend or loved one who has suffered a sports injury shows any signs of depression or loss of interest in activities once loved, weight loss or gain, restlessness, or mental or physical fatigue, urge him or her to talk to a health-care professional about feelings and talk to a parent or counselor right away; if left untreated, depression can lead to suicide.
- One of the best things you can do to help your friend or loved one is to be there for him or her to listen, talk, and get out of the house with positive activities such as going to the movies, taking a walk (if he or she is able), and spending time with other friends.

14 |||

Paying for Care

Bill, 17, twisted his ankle during his last soccer game.
Immediately, his ankle swelled and turned black and blue, forcing Bill to sit out the second half of the game. Several days later, Bill's ankle is still quite sore and swollen, and he's having trouble putting weight on it. Bill is hesitant to go to the doctor, however, because due to his father's layoff, his family doesn't currently have health insurance. So he's hoping the injury will heal on its own.

Despite his fears about the cost of his treatment, Bill should seek medical attention as soon as possible. His ankle is very likely broken and requires treatment by a medical professional. If he ignores the ankle, it could lead to a permanent injury that may prevent him from playing soccer ever again. Even though his family doesn't currently have health insurance, there are ways that Bill can be treated without having to pay the medical bills himself.

Not having health insurance—or not having enough health insurance—can be a scary and worrisome situation for teens and their parents. Luckily, there are many options out there to help you get the coverage you need. This chapter will help uninsured or underinsured teen athletes like Bill to understand the free and subsidized health-care services that are available to them, as well as how they can take advantage of these services.

WHO PAYS FOR HEALTH CARE?

When you go to a doctor's office or hospital for treatment, most of the cost of the services is paid by your health insurance company. Until you are a young adult, if your parents have health insurance, you will be covered under their plan. When you become an independent adult living on your own, you will get health insurance on your own, probably through your employer.

Unfortunately, as Bill's story illustrates, not everyone has health insurance. Health-care coverage has become a problem for many Americans. When unexpected and potentially costly situations come up like Bill's, the situation can be scary.

But luckily, there are a number of things that Bill and other teenagers in the same situation can do to get the health-care coverage necessary—for unexpected injuries and routine care.

WHERE TO GO FOR EMERGENCY CARE

If you do not have health insurance and you find yourself in a situation like Bill's, it's true that going to see a doctor can be very expensive. However, know that if you suffer a sports injury that requires emergency treatment, you will be examined and treated at an emergency room, even if you don't have insurance or cannot pay for the services.

If your situation is not a medical emergency, but you still need prompt treatment, talk with your health-care provider about possibly getting a discount (often called a sliding scale) or setting up a payment plan. These days, this is not an uncommon practice, so you shouldn't feel embarrassed about it.

GENERAL HEALTH-CARE COVERAGE

In the United States, you can obtain health insurance through your employer, your parents' employer, or your university. Many people have to buy health insurance on their own.

These days, more and more families and individuals are finding themselves in a situation similar to Bill's. For some, the main breadwinner has been laid off, and fewer and fewer employers are offering health insurance as a benefit. Other families simply can't afford health insurance or the high deductibles or co-pays (portions of the fee for service) that go along with it.

Thankfully, most families like Bill's have options. Every state in the nation now has a program specifically for infants, children, and teenagers in need of health insurance coverage called "Insure Kids Now." This program covers doctors' visits, prescription medications, and other necessary medical services for little or no cost.

The specific eligibility rules vary, but most states will cover unin-sured kids ages 18 or younger whose families earn $34,100 or less per year for a family of four. For more information, or to research whether or not your family is eligible, go to www.insurekidsnow. gov or call 1-877-KIDS-NOW.

If you or your family is below a certain income limit and you do not have health insurance, another option for you is Medicaid. Medicaid is a state-run public health program that covers a variety of health-care services. In all states, Medicaid covers hospital and outpatient care, home health services, and doctors' visits. In some states, a co-pay is required for certain services. For more information on Medicaid and to find out whether you or your family are eligible, go to the Medicaid Web site at www.CMS.gov.

In addition, the following sites will help you find low-cost health care in your area:

Actors' Health Insurance Resource Center. Originally created in 1998 by the Actors' Fund of America as a health insurance resource for people in the entertainment industry, the Actors' Health Insurance Resource Center (AHIRC) has now expanded to include resources for the uninsured, the underinsured, self-employed people, and low-income workers. It is a great online resource for finding leads to affordable, quality health insurance. www.ahirc.org

Cover the Uninsured Guide to Finding Health Insurance in Your State. An excellent source of leads to health-care options in your area, the Cover the Uninsured Web site offers a state-by-state information page and is available in both English and Spanish. www. covertheuninsuredweek.org/stateguides.

The Health Assistance Partnership. The Health Assistance Part-nership (www.healthassistancepartnership.org) provides information regarding legal rights to treatment and free information on Medicare, Medicare drug coverage, Medicaid, low-income health benefits, sup-plemental coverage, and long-term care.

The Hill-Burton Program. You are eligible for care under the Hill-Burton Program if your family's income falls below the national poverty lines, which in 2008 was $21,200 per year for a family of four in all states except Alaska and Hawaii (where it is higher). www.hrsa. gov/hillburton/default.htm.

INFORMATION ON COVERAGE FOR MEDICATIONS

Some sports injuries require medication as part of their treatment, be it pain medication, steroids, cortisone, anti-inflammatories, or other types of drugs. If you have health insurance with prescription coverage, these medications may be paid for by your insurance company. If you do not have prescription coverage, however, and you need medication, ask your doctor to prescribe the cheapest drug that will work for you (called a "generic" drug).

In addition, some pharmaceutical companies such as Pfizer and Eli Lilly & Company offer free medications to people who cannot afford them. To apply for these free medications, you will need a note from your doctor that states the reason you need the medication, as well as a statement declaring that your family has no prescription coverage for the medication and inadequate financial resources to pay for it out-of-pocket.

To find out which pharmaceutical companies offer free medications, check out the individual companies' Web sites. To find other patient assistant programs that offer free prescription medications to those in need, look at the following Web sites:

Free Medicine Foundation
www.freemedicinefoundation.com
The Free Medicine Foundation is a volunteer-run program that helps families like Bill's eliminate or significantly lower their prescription medication costs. The program helps members save hundreds of dollars per year on each medication they take. The Free Medicine Foundation works by helping people get free medicine directly from pharmaceutical sponsors. If your family currently has no prescription coverage, maxed-out prescription benefits, or a low income, you are eligible to apply. Families who qualify for free medications have incomes ranging from the poverty level to $84,800. However, each sponsored drug has its own eligibility criteria.

NeedyMeds Program
www.needymeds.org
A database of patient assistance programs, the NeedyMeds program helps people obtain health supplies, medications,

and medical equipment. The site was created by Libby Overly, M.Ed., MSW, a former social worker from Alabama, and Richard J. Sagall, M.D., in 1997, and it is constantly being updated with new information. NeedyMeds recently added a free clinics database to its Web site and started an online forum, NeedyMeds Forums, for patient advocates.

Partnership for Prescription Assistance
https://www.pparx.org/Intro.php
The Partnership for Prescription Assistance is a group of doctors, community groups, pharmaceutical companies, patient
advocacy organizations, and other health-care providers
that helps patients without prescription coverage to get the
medications they need. The organization matches people
who are eligible for free or subsidized medications with
the public and private programs that can help them. Some
of the specific organizations involved with the Partnership
include the American Academy of Family Physicians, the
National Alliance for Hispanic Health, the National Association for the Advancement of Colored People (NAACP),
and the National Medical Association.

RxAssist
www.rxassist.org
RxAssist is a comprehensive database of patient assistance
programs run by pharmaceutical companies that helps people who can't afford medication to obtain free medicines.
The site also offers articles to help health-care professionals
and patients find necessary information, relevant news, and
practical tools.

MEDICATIONS FROM CANADA
As prescription health-care coverage becomes more of an issue in the United States, there is more and more buzz about people buying their drugs from Canada. Although the U.S. government frowns on the practice, partially because there is no way to regulate the Canadian drugs and assure they are safe, many consumer advocates say Canada is an economical resource for expensive medications. If you and your parents decide to try to buy medications from Canada, make sure you are using a reputable source. As the practice of buying medications from Canada becomes more popular, several states have developed programs to help their residents obtain Canadian medications safely.

The following states have set up programs to help their residents obtain lower-priced prescription medications from other countries:

Minnesota. The governor of Minnesota set up a Web site called Minnesota RXConnect online (http://www.state.mn.us/portal/mn/jsp/home.do?agency=Rx) to help residents obtain discounted drugs from both Canada and the United Kingdom.

New Hampshire. New Hampshire offers a few different Web sites to help residents find discounted medications abroad, including a link to CanadaDrugs.com. For more information, go to www.egov.nh.gov/medicine%2Dcabinet.

North Dakota. The following Web site provides North Dakota residents with links to Web sites that import discounted medications from abroad: http://www.nd.gov/content.htm?parentCatID=91&id=Prescription.

WHAT YOU NEED TO KNOW

> Not having health insurance—or not having enough health insurance—can be a scary and worrisome situation for teens and their parents. Luckily, there are many options out there to help you get the coverage you need.

> If you suffer a sports injury that requires emergency treatment, you will be examined and treated at an emergency room, even if you don't have insurance or cannot pay for the services.

> If your situation is not a medical emergency, but you still need prompt treatment and do not have insurance, talk with your health-care provider about possibly getting a discount or setting up a payment plan.

> Every state in the nation now has a program specifically for infants, children, and teenagers in need of health insurance coverage called "Insure Kids Now." This program covers doctors' visits, prescription medications and other necessary medical services for little or no cost. For more information, or to research whether or not your family is eligible, go to www.insurekidsnow.gov or call 1-877-KIDS-NOW.

> If you or your family is below a certain income limit and you do not have health insurance, another option for you is Medicaid, a state-run public health program that covers a variety of health-care services. For more information on Medicaid and

to find out whether you or your family are eligible, go to the Medicaid Web site at www.CMS.gov.

▸ Some pharmaceutical companies such as Pfizer and Eli Lilly & Company offer free medications to people who cannot afford them. To apply for these free medications, you will need a note from your doctor that states the reason you need the medication, as well as a statement declaring that your family has no prescription coverage for the medication and inadequate financial resources to pay for it out-of-pocket.

APPENDIX

Associations

American Academy of Family Physicians
www.familydoctor.org

American Academy of Orthopedic Surgeons
www.aaos.org

American Academy of Pediatrics
www.aap.org

American Academy of Podiatric Sports Medicine
www.aapsm.org

American College of Sports Medicine
www.acsm.org

American Orthopaedic Society for Sports Medicine
www.sportsmed.org

Institute for Preventive Sports Medicine
http://members.aol.com/wwwipsm/index.html

Kids Health
www.kidshealth.org

Mayo Clinic
www.mayoclinic.com

Med Web Sports Medicine
http://www.medweb.emory.edu/medweb

National Institute of Arthritis and Musculoskeletal and Skin Diseases
www.niams.nih.gov

Physician and Sportsmedicine
http://www.physsportsmed.com

GLOSSARY

abrasion Any injury that rubs off the surface of the skin.

aerobic activity Sustained activity that increases the heart rate, strengthening the cardiovascular system.

acromioclavicular (AC) joint The joint that joins the scapula and clavicle (collarbone).

acute injuries Injuries that result from a sudden trauma.

adductor muscles The muscles of the inner thigh.

anaerobic activity Short-duration exercise that does not use oxygen.

anterior cruciate ligament (ACL) The ligament that runs from the top to the bottom of the knee joint, essentially holding the joint together.

Bankart lesion An injury to part of the shoulder joint called the **labrum,** a cuff of **cartilage** that forms a cup that the **humerus** (arm bone) moves within.

blowout fracture Fracture to the bones surrounding the eyeball.

boxer's fracture A break of the bones of the hand that form the knuckles.

burner A sudden burning pain and a feeling of weakness that shoots down one arm. Also called a stinger.

bruise Swelling or bleeding in a muscle or other soft body tissue.

bursitis Inflammation of a bursa, a tiny fluid-filled sac that functions as a gliding surface to reduce friction between tissues of the body; frequently in the shoulder.

burst fracture When a trauma causes the vertebrae in the spine to literally burst apart and shatter.

cartilage A tough, stretchy tissue that covers the ends of bones to form a low-friction, shock-absorbing surface for joints.

cauliflower ear A common injury in wrestlers, cauliflower ear occurs when the ear is frequently bent over or punched during wrestling holds. As a result, blood pools under the skin, and the ear swells, taking on the appearance of a cauliflower.

chronic exertional compartment syndrome An exercise-induced condition that causes pain, swelling, and sometimes disability in affected muscles of the arms or legs.

chronic pain Pain that persists.

clavicle Collarbone.

compression fracture A fracture of a vertebra in the back of the spine.

computed tomography scan (CT scan) A test that produces images of the body that show variations in the density of different types of tissue.

concussion A violent jarring or shock to the head that causes a temporary jolt to the brain, usually resulting from a blow to the head or a fall.

congenital hip dysplasia A malformation of the hip joint, where the ball at the top of the thighbone isn't stable in its socket.

dehydration A deficit in body fluids.

delayed onset muscle soreness (DOMS) Muscle soreness that sets in 24 to 72 hours after strenuous exercise and subsides within two to three days.

disc A fibrous pillow that acts as shock absorbers for the spine.

dislocation Displacement of a body part.

exercise-induced anaphylaxis A syndrome in which athletes experience symptoms of anaphylaxis—a severe whole-body allergic reaction—after increased physical activity.

exercise-induced asthma A condition that involves difficulty breathing associated with exercise.

fracture A crack or break in a bone.

Freiberg infraction A painful collapse of the joint surface of the second metatarsal head.

growth plate injuries Also called apophysitis, one type of stress injury that is particularly prevalent in young athletes is to the growth areas of the long bones in the arms and legs, and occasionally the hands and feet.

heat exhaustion A potentially serious condition that results from prolonged exposure to high temperatures. Symptoms include nausea, dizziness, weakness, headache, heavy perspiration, pale and moist skin, dilated pupils, low body temperature, weak pulse, fainting, and disorientation.

heat stroke Medical emergency that results when the body's internal thermostat fails to keep the body cool, causing body temperature to rise up to 108 degrees Fahrenheit.

high ankle sprain An ankle sprain that involves injury to the large ligament above the ankle that joins together the two bones of the lower leg.

Hill-Sachs lesion A divot of the **humerus** (arm bone) that gets injured during a shoulder dislocation.

hip pointer A bruise on the pelvis caused by a direct blow to a hip bone.

humerus The bone between the shoulder and the elbow.

hyperextension When a joint bends too far the wrong way.

hyponatremia The opposite of dehydration, when the sodium in your blood becomes diluted from drinking too much water.

iliotibial band (ITB) Part of a tough muscle on the outside of the thigh and knee that runs from the lower part of the quadriceps to the bottom of the knee joint.

iontophoresis A procedure that involves painting a cortisone solution on the skin and then driving it into the tendon using an electric current.

labrum A ring of fibrous cartilage around the edge of the articular (joint) surface of a bone.

laceration An irregular tearlike wound due to some form of blunt trauma.

lateral collateral ligament (LCL) A tight band of tissue that travels up the outside of the knee.

lateral ankle sprain A sprain of the ligaments on the outside of your ankle.

lateral epicondylitis (tennis elbow) A repetitive use injury of the tendon that extends the wrist through the muscles of the forearm and attaches to the outer (lateral) elbow.

ligament strain Often referred to as a "pull," the stretching or tearing of a ligament, for example, a pulled hamstring or back.

Lisfranc complex An area of the mid-foot, where a cluster of small bones forms an arch on top of the foot.

Little League elbow A group of elbow problems related to the stress of pitching and throwing in young athletes.

magnetic resonance imaging (MRI) A test using a magnetic field through which pulses of radio frequency radiation are projected that can show differences in tissue and bone structure.

maximum heart rate The maximum number of times your heart can beat each minute; to find your maximum heart rate, subtract your age from the number 220.

medial ankle sprain An ankle sprain that stresses the inside ligament of the ankle; in many cases, rather than becoming sprained itself, it pulls off a piece of bone where it attaches.

medial collateral ligament (MCL) A tight band of tissue that spans the knee joint on the inner side of the knee.

medial epicondylitis (golfer's elbow) Pain and inflammation on the inner side of the elbow, where the tendons of the forearm muscles attach to the bump on the inside of the elbow.

medial tibial stress syndrome The sleeve of tissue surrounding the **tibia** becomes inflamed due to repeated stress.

meniscus A piece of cartilage in the knee located at the junction of the two bones in the knee joint.

metatarsal bones The long, thin bones that run from the top of the foot to the toes.

Morton's foot A foot that has a second toe that is longer than the first toe.

muscle spasm Tightness in the muscle that results from intense exercise

nonsteroidal anti-inflammatory medications Medications that relieve pain, swelling, stiffness, and inflammation.

obedience coaches Coaches who run their teams with themselves in charge.

olecranon bursitis (Popeye elbow) Condition characterized by pain, swelling, and inflammation of the olecranon bursa located in the elbow.

Osgood-Schlatter syndrome A painful condition that affects growing children and teenagers. The pain comes from the growth plate of the bump on the leg just below the kneecap, called the tibial tubercle.

osteitis pubis Inflammation of the area where the right and left pubic bones meet in the front of the pelvis.

osteochondral fractures Cartilage injuries.

overuse injuries Injuries that occur over a period of time and result from sports that involve prolonged, repetitive motions or impacts. Also called chronic injuries.

patella Kneecap.

patellofemoral syndrome (runner's knee) Pain at the front of the knee.

Perthes disease A condition that causes necrosis of the femoral head (ball) that fits into the socket in the hip joint.

pitcher's elbow Pain and disability associated with the tearing of tendons from their attachment on the epicondyle of the **humerus** often with involvement of tissues within and around the elbow; this injury is often found in pitchers.

plantar fascia An elastic band on the sole of the foot that helps hold up the arch. It runs from the heel bone to the toes, and it helps absorb shock.

post-concussion syndrome A complex disorder in which concussion symptoms such as headaches and dizziness last for weeks and sometimes months after the impact that caused the concussion.

posterior cruciate ligament (PCL) A ligament that prevents the **tibia** from sliding backward under the femur.

posterolateral corner A junction of muscles and ligaments in the knee that help it flex.

pre-participation exam (pre-part exam) A physical examination athletes undergo before starting a sports season. The exam is meant to point out your strengths and weaknesses and to identify any conditions that might make playing a sport unsafe for you.

pronation Feet that roll inward.

responsibility coaches Coaches who put more responsibility on student athletes, and they give them more say in the way the team functions.

rhabdomyolysis A breakdown of muscle fibers into the bloodstream that can lead to kidney damage.

ringworm A fungal skin infection that lives on the dead tissues of the skin, hair, and nails.

scapula Shoulder blade.

Scheuermann's disease A condition that occurs when the upper part of the spine doesn't grow as fast as the back part of the spine.

Sever's disease A **growth plate injury** of the heel.

skier's thumb A tear of the ulnar collateral ligament of the metacarpophalangeal joint of the thumb. Also called gamekeeper's thumb.

slipped capital femoral epiphysis (SCFE) A condition that occurs in children in which the growing end of the femur (thighbone) slips from the ball of the hip joint.

spondylolisthesis A condition in which one of the vertebrae of the spine slips out of place onto the vertebra below it.

spondylolysis A stress fracture of the part of the vertebrae that connect the front and rear portions of the bone.

sports hernia A tear in the muscles of the lower abdomen that can cause the muscle to pull away from the bones of the hip.

sprain An acute injury to the ligaments surrounding a joint such as the ankle or wrist.

strain An injury to a muscle or tendon.

stress fracture Tiny cracks or weak spots that appear on the surface of a bone when excessive stress is placed on the bone.

subluxation A partial dislocation.

supination Feet that roll outward.

target heart rate Recommended intensity level for cardio-respiratory exercise.

tendonitis The irritation, inflammation, and swelling of a tendon that results from repetitive stretching/straining.

tibia Shinbone.

transverse process The bony protrusion on either side of the arch of a vertebra.

ulnar collateral ligament (UCL) A ligament that helps stabilize the elbow. It is composed of three bands—the anterior, posterior, and transverse bands—and it spans from the ulna (a bone in the forearm) to the **humerus** (the bone of the upper arm).

whiplash A neck injury caused by a trauma that leads to an abrupt flexion/extension motion of the neck.

READ MORE ABOUT IT

"Acute Finger Injuries: Part I. Tendons and Ligaments." American Family Physician. URL: http://www.aafp.org/afp/20060301/810.html. Accessed June 25, 2009.

"Adolescent Elbow Injuries In Baseball." ACC Athletics Baseball. URL: http://www.theacc.com/sports/m-basebl/spec-rel/033105aag.html. Accessed June 25, 2009.

"Boxer's Fracture." EMedicineHealth.com. URL: http://www.emedicine health.com/boxers_fracture/article_em.htm. Accessed June 25, 2009.

"Connecting with your coach." TeensHealth, the Nemours Foundation. URL: http://kidshealth.org/teen/food_fitness/sports/coach_relationships.html. Accessed June 25, 2009.

"Dealing with sports injuries." TeensHealth, the Nemours Foundation (June 2007). URL: http://kidshealth.org/teen/food_fitness/sports/sports_injuries.html. Accessed June 25, 2009.

"Elbow fractures and dislocations." EMedicineHealth.com. URL: http://emedicine.medscape.com/article/389069-overview. Accessed June 25, 2009.

"Exercise-induced anaphylaxis." EMedicineHealth.com. URL: http://emedicine.medscape.com/article/886641-overview. Accessed June 25, 2009.

"Fractures in children." Cincinnati Children's. URL: http://www.cincinnatichildrens.org/health/info/orthopaedics/diagnose/fractures.htm. Accessed June 25, 2009.

"Freiberg Infraction." EMedicineHealth.com. URL: http://emedicine.medscape.com/article/1236085-overview. Accessed June 25, 2009.

"Golfer's elbow." The Mayo Clinic. URL: http://www.mayoclinic.com/health/golfers-elbow/DS00713/DSECTION = preventionv. Accessed June 25, 2009.

Gotlin, D. O., Robert S., ed. *Sports Injuries Guidebook*. Champaign, Ill.: Human Kinetics, 2007.

"Growth plate injuries." Medical College of Wisconsin. URL: http://healthlink.mcw.edu/article/926048658.html. Accessed June 25, 2009.

Guyer, Ruth Levy, Ph.D. "Sports Injuries: In Your Face." The National Institutes of Health Office of Science Education. URL: http://science-education.nih.gov/home2.nsf/Educational + ResourcesResource + FormatsOnline + Resources + High + School/26DA3B19E6E78D 3685256CCD0071BF9F. Accessed June 25, 2009.

"Hand and Wrist Injuries: Part I. Nonemergent Evaluation." American Family Physician. URL: http://www.aafp.org/afp/20040415/1941. html. Accessed June 25, 2009.

"Head injuries." MassGeneral Hospital for Children. URL: http://www. massgeneral.org/children/adolescenthealth/articles/aa_head_injuries. aspx. Accessed June 25, 2009.

"Herpes Gladiatorum Is Common Among Wrestlers." WebMD Health News. URL: http://www.webmd.com/fitness-exercise/news/20000110/ herpes-wrestlers. Accessed June 25, 2009.

"Impetigo." TeensHealth, The Nemours Foundation. URL: http://kids health.org/parent/infections/bacterial_viral/impetigo.html. Accessed June 25, 2009.

"Infectious disease outbreaks in competitive sports." AJSM Preview. URL: http://74.125.47.132/search?q = cache:Fwc4OaFlcwQJ:www. ccar-ccra.com/english/pdfs/Outbre aksInSportsAJSM06.pdf + infectio us + diseases + contact + sports + teens&hl = en&ct = clnk&cd = 11&gl = us. Accessed June 25, 2009.

"Keep injured high school athletes out of the game." The American Academy of Orthopedic Surgeons. URL: http://orthoinfo.aaos.org/topic. cfm?topic = A00048. Accessed June 25, 2009.

"Kids and sports injuries." CBC News. URL: http://www.cbc.ca/news/ yourinterview/2008/05/kids_and_sports_injuries.html. Accessed June 25, 2009.

"Knocked out tooth." The Children, Youth and Women's Health Service. URL: http://www.cyh.com/HealthTopics/HealthTopicDetails.aspx?p = 243&np = 292&id = 2353. Accessed June 25, 2009.

"Legg-Calve-Perthes Disease." URL: http://www.pediatric-orthopedics. com/Topics/Perthes/perthes.html. Accessed June 25, 2009.

Levy, Allan M., and Mark L. Fuerst. "Sports Injury Handbook: Professional Advice for Amateur Athletes." New York: John Wiley and Sons, 1993.

"Lisfranc (Midfoot) Fracture." The American Academy of Orthopedic Surgeons. URL: http://orthoinfo.aaos.org/topic.cfm?topic = A00162. Accessed June 25, 2009.

"Lisfranc Injury of the Foot: A Commonly Missed Diagnosis." The American Academy of Family Physicians. URL: http://www.aafp.org/ afp/980700ap/burrough.html. Accessed June 25, 2009.

"Orthopedics & Sports Medicine Frequently Asked Questions." The Lexington Clinic. URL: http://www.lcsportsmed.com/faq.htm#question3. Accessed June 25, 2009.

"Pain Relief for Common Pediatric Sports Injuries." Children's Healthcare of Atlanta. 2009. URL: http://www.choa.org/default.aspx?id = 1462. Accessed June 25, 2009.

"Patellar tendon rupture. EMedicineHealth.com. URL: http://emedicine. medscape.com/article/1249472-overview. Accessed June 25, 2009.

"Prevention of exercise and sports-related injury, part 1. Palo Alto Medical Foundation. URL: http://www.pamf.org/sports/chen/sportsinjury. html. Accessed June 25, 2009.

"Return to play." The American Academy of Orthopedic Surgeons. URL: http://orthoinfo.aaos.org/topic.cfm?topic = A00365. Accessed June 25, 2009.

"Ringworm." TeensHealth, The Nemours Foundation. URL: http://kids health.org/teen/infections/fungal/ringworm.html. Accessed June 25, 2009.

"Should I exercise with a cold?" URL: http://sportsmedicine.about.com/ cs/injuryprevention/a/aa011402a.htm. Accessed June 25, 2009.

"Sporting injuries: feeling them." Children, youth, and women's health service. URL: http://www.cyh.com/HealthTopics/HealthTopicDetails. aspx?p = 243&np = 292&id = 2448. Accessed June 25, 2009.

"Sports Injuries." The National Institute of Arthritis and Musculoskeletal and Skin Diseases. URL: http://www.niams.nih.gov/Health_Info/ Sports_Injuries/child_sports_injuries.asp. Accessed June 25, 2009.

"Sports injuries a growing problem in kids." The American Academy of Pediatrics. URL: http://www.aap.org/advocacy/releases/sportsinjury. htm. Accessed June 25, 2009.

"Sports injury prevention." The University of Virginia. URL: http://www. healthsystem.virginia.edu/uvahealth/peds_orthopaedics/prevent.cfm. Accessed June 25, 2009.

"Staying in the game: Preventing sports injuries in children and teens." Akron Childrens' Hospital. URL: https://www.akronchildrens.org/ cms/site/8c701a8f1559a0dc/index.html/. Accessed June 25, 2009.

"Slipped capital femoral epiphysis." FamilyDoctor.org. URL: http:// familydoctor.org/online/famdocen/home/children/parents/special/ bone/282.html. Accessed June 25, 2009.

"Spondylolysis and Spondylolisthesis." American Academy of Orthopedic Surgeons. URL: http://orthoinfo.aaos.org/topic.cfm?topic = a00053. Accessed June 25, 2009.

"Teen sports: safety first." FamilyEducation.com. URL: http://life.family education.com/teen/safety/48514.html. Accessed June 25, 2009.

"Testicular Torsion." UrologyChannel.com. URL: http://www.urology channel.com/emergencies/torsion.shtml. Accessed June 25, 2009.

"Types of growth plate injuries." URL: http://www.wrongdiagnosis.com/ g/growth_plate_injuries/subtypes.htm. Accessed June 25, 2009.

"What is a high ankle sprain?" URL: http://orthopedics.about.com/od/ sprainsstrains/a/syndesmosis.htm. Accessed June 25, 2009.

"What is a hip flexor strain?" University Sports Medicine, Buffalo. URL: http://www.ubsportsmed.buffalo.edu/education/hipflexor.html. Accessed June 25, 2009.

"When can teens return to sports after a head injury?" by Denise Garvey, M.D. The UCLA Department of Medicine. URL: http://www.med.ucla. edu/modules/wfsection/article.php?articleid = 167. Accessed June 25, 2009.

INDEX

194

tibia fracture
  acute 131
  stress 128–129
tibial tuberosity 120
tinea corporis (ringworm) 150, 155–156, 159, 166
toenail, black 145
toe raise 132
toe touch 100–101
tooth loss 38, 150, 157
torn cartilage. *See* cartilage injuries
torus fractures 81
transmissible diseases 159
trapezius muscle 50, 52
trauma. *See* acute injuries
traumatic brain injury, mild. *See* concussion
treatment 7–8. *See also specific injuries*
triangular fibrocartilage complex (TFCC) 80
triceps curl 74
triceps muscle 61
triceps tendonitis 67
turf toe 144–145
twisted testicle 150, 154–155, 161
Tylenol (acetaminophen) 27

U

UCL. *See* ulnar collateral ligament of elbow; ulnar collateral ligament of hand
ulna 61, 77
ulnar collateral ligament (UCL) of elbow
  anatomy of 66
  injuries of 66–67, 169
ulnar collateral ligament (UCL) of hand, injuries of 84–86
ulnar fracture 78
ulnar nerve 77
ulnohumeral joint 61
ultrasound
  diagnostic. *See specific injuries*
  therapeutic 10, 49

V

vertebra fracture
  burst 99
  compression 98–99
  stress 91–92, 96–97
vertebra slippage 91–92, 96–97, 101, 166
volar plate injury 87–88
volleyball 168

W

wall push-ups 52
wall sit 132
warm up 4
water intake 6, 23
weight lifting 46, 68. *See also* strength training
whiplash 41–42
wrestling 165–166
wrist cartilage 80
wrist curl 73–74, 89
wrist exercises 89
wrist fracture 78–80, 89–90
wrist injuries 76–80, 88–90
  anatomical considerations in 77
  gymnastic 167
  prevention of 88
  teen vulnerability to 76
wrist sprain 77–78, 89, 167
wrist subluxation 77–78
wrist tendonitis 80

X

X-rays 27

Y

yoga lotus stretch 116